Considering Venus

D. GISELE ISAAC

Library of Congress Cataloging-in-Publication Data

Considering Venus: a novel by D. Gisele Isaac. — 2nd ed.
p. cm
ISBN 1-885778-42-2

Seaburn Publishing
PO Box 2085
Astoria, New York 11102
www.seaburn.com
                                        zip:/S0462

Manufactured in the United States of America
10 9 8 7 6 5 4 3 2 1

WHAT READERS ARE SAYING

A great piece of literary effort...
— Paedeia Reviews, NY

• • • •

Congratulations on a book well done, I'm sure u will do it again with a BANG!
Remember your audience is waiting for the sequel.
GOOD LUck

• • • •

Wonderful and captivating. You'll wonder "what-if?"
A truly delightful read. So strong were the character developments that I too
wanted to call Cass while she was in Antigua. Where's the sequel?

• • • •

Arguably the single most interesting book I've ever read... It's about a 'normal'
woman following her heart inspite of what her head and her family sometimes
have to say about her life, and the heartache that accompanies making unpopu-
lar choices.

• • • •

A brave literary work by a fist time novelist...
To be a Woman. To be Black. To be Gay.
Ms. Isaac undertook a difficult task in dealing with a rather controversial sub-
ject, obviously a social situation that requires critical thinking and unbiased
analysis of human emotions vis-à-vis social biases. She manages all that in her
book, and more, with sensitivity and expertise. Without polemics or preach-
ing, her understanding of her subject and skillful writing leave the reader with
a sense of profound compassion and responsibility. I found it hard to put the
book down.

• • • •

We still have a problem understanding why this book is not in the movies
yet...
— Black Book News Magazine

• • • •

The question that society continues to ask and scientists continue to seek for
explanations is, can two people of the same sex meet, fall in love and determine
to live as happily as they can?
Read Considering Venus and watch yourself emerge from a closet that you
never thought existed...

Chris McMahon,
— The Gazette

sisted, it was a blessing, because he had been in so much pain.

She spoke quickly, dispassionately, as though she'd said this many times before. But Cass was accustomed to hurt's many disguises, and she recognized the pain beneath Lesley's words.

"Tell me about him," she encouraged, covering Lesley's limp hand.

Lesley was startled. Usually, people clucked a brief word of sympathy and hurried on, as though she had put them in an awkward position. She was startled, but grateful.

"Gene was a good man," she began, a little defensively, "and I'm not just saying that because he's gone, mind you. He was good to me and to his kids."

She had married Gene straight out of high school because he was going off to Vietnam, she said. Lesley described her husband as a hard worker and a conscientious man who had provided a comfortable life and a loving environment for the family. The time he spent in Vietnam had helped to make him a curious combination of tough survivalist and tender family man. Because they had not had much time to get to really know each other before he went away, Lesley recounted wistfully, he had tried to make their marriage a courtship and he also worked hard at being a good father.

She had a daughter, Generes, and two sons, Dow and Seth. Lesley described her kids in that understated, matter-of-fact way mothers adopt when they're trying not to seem boastful. Generes lived in Miami and was a flight attendant, Lesley said. She'd left college after two years, deciding she wanted to see the world before she became tied down with a family. Dow was a mathematical whiz who had landed a job on Wall Street right after his graduation from Baruch; he lived in the City and visited her every two weeks or so. And Seth was a senior at St. John's where he, too, was majoring in math.

"The kids are pretty good," Lesley mused, "but they've got their own lives, you know. They call all the time and visit often, especially Seth, since he's in Queens, but to tell the truth, it's terribly lonely sometimes."

Watching Lesley talk was like observing light come slowly into a previously shuttered room, Cass thought. Her face became animated and she gestured when she spoke, squinting her long, narrow eyes. Her voice was low, with a conspiratorial quality that drew you in, made you listen to her. And gazing at that mouth, the lips expanding and contracting, Cass wondered why she had never paid attention to Lesley in school. "Oh my word! Look how late it is," Lesley exclaimed, as though sensing Cass's disengagement. "I've been talking and talking for so long. I really didn't mean to keep you."

"From what?" Cass inquired, dragging herself back from her contemplation. "It was a pleasure for me. And what's the rush, anyway?" She looked at her watch and shrugged. "Why don't you come home with me for a little while? It's barely 8:00 o'clock, it's Saturday night, and you said the house was lonely."

Lesley let herself be persuaded, but in the cab uptown she was quiet, wondering if, perhaps, she had capitulated too easily, opened up too much. Sure, she had known Cassandra since high school, but they hadn't exactly been friends and she didn't want to impose on her any more than she already had.

I really need to get out more, Lesley fretted, and not keep myself so closed off. But get out where? And with whom? Only last week I had to spend my birthday with Seth and his girlfriend. She'd been so grateful for their company she'd taken *them* out to dinner.

When Gene was alive they used to have a circle of friends out on the Island: three other couples with whom they bowled every week after dinner and whose kids had played with theirs. During his illness they had been very supportive. Ginny, who had no children, had even slept over to help Lesley on Gene's worst nights. The other women had cooked or shopped, while the men regularly came over to keep Gene company. But as the months after the funeral wore on, she realized that she saw them less and less often, although they occasionally called. She had been invited to a couple of summer barbecues and graduation parties, but Lesley felt, essentially, on the fringe.

Having read about and discussed this particular situation in her sociology classes, she was not angry, not even hurt. She understood that as friends, they were couples first and foremost, and, by herself, she didn't quite have a place.

It was true that she got along well with the women on her job, but because she drove in to Brooklyn it was hard to maintain after-work friendships. Lesley sighed.

Cass grabbed her arm. "Hey, don't leave me now," she warned

jokingly. "You were just getting thawed out, back there. Whatever it is you're worrying about, drop it for tonight, won't you?"

Lesley squeezed the hand that gripped her. "You're right."

The cab slowed to a stop on 83rd Street and Columbus. Cass paid the fare and they walked into a smart building where she greeted the doorman by name.

Stepping into Cass's apartment, Lesley forgot it was almost fall. Directly across from the front door hung a large Haitian painting, vividly colored, of a buxom woman suckling twin infants. On the west wall, two beautifully framed photographs of white-sand beaches, one at sunset and the other at sunrise, flanked a gold sunburst mirror. Valances in a bright Madras print sat like head wraps atop the wide wooden blinds, the pattern being repeated in the half-dozen or so cushions that were grouped on the parchment-colored couch. The hardwood floor was partially covered by a well-preserved wool rug in burnt sienna, in the middle of which stood a glass-topped table, crowned by a pot of gloriously colored tropical crotons.

"Oh, my word!"Lesley exclaimed in delight. "Wherever did you get that?"

"My mother gave me that plant on one of my trips home, and I've managed to confuse it into thinking it's still in the Caribbean," Cass said in a satisfied tone.

"This is such a beautiful apartment," Lesley said, as her eyes took in Cass's collection of enamel, porcelain, crystal and jade fish and the family photos in red and amber frames that were grouped on a pair of console tables. The apartment was warm, personal, welcoming.

"I would love to spend the whole winter here," Lesley sighed longingly.

Flashing her gap-toothed smile, Cass asked, "And who says you can't?"

4

They discussed the convention and the state of public education in New York City, each telling the other about the challenges and rewards of her job and comparing current trends with their school days.

Rummaging around in a closet Cass found their high-school yearbook, and from the safe distance of 25 years they laughed at the faces, hairstyles and quirks of classmates and discussed the teachers they had loved and hated. Cass had a gift for mimicry and when she got up and switched across the room like Miss Soto, their Spanish teacher, Lesley laughed until she had to rush to the bathroom.

Later that night, sharing two bottles of wine, they relived their youth through Cass's record collection. Cass had always found company in music, especially during her solitary high-school years, and she had learned all the words to the songs and had mastered all the moves.

Cass sang along with the Jones Girls at the top of her voice, "You gon-na make me love somebody else, if you keep on treating me the way you do," while Lesley brought up the rear, "I don't wanna do it! I don't wanna do it!"

Cass pulled Lesley up from the couch, effortlessly swinging her from the pop exuberance of Archie Bell and The Drells' "Tighten Up" into the funk of Joe Tex's "Ain't Gonna Bump No More With No Big Fat Woman." After an exhausting session, they both sank to the floor and, with eyes closed, harmonized on Billy Paul's "Me and Mrs. Jones" then Cass's favorite, "When Will I See You Again?" by The Three Degrees.

"Ah," Cass sighed, turning toward her guest, "when music was music. Next time I'll play you some calypso. My father gave me quite a collection and I've added to it considerably over the years."

Sweaty and hungry, they drifted into the kitchen to forage for food. Lesley insisted on whipping up scrambled eggs with bacon, and they lingered over their plates, talking about this and that until they began to yawn.

With typical Caribbean generosity, Cass invited Lesley to stay the night, brushing aside her protests and changing the bed linens in record time. Secretly relieved at not having to take the train at that time, Lesley accepted. Showered and wearing a borrowed Betty Boop sleepshirt, she fell into bed.

Around midday she woke with a feeling of well-being. For the first time in many months, her first thought was not about the empty space beside her. She felt rested, refreshed, even anticipatory. She performed her ablutions and went in search of Cass, whom she found setting the table.

"Good afternoon," Cass said, pointedly but smiling. "So, how'd you sleep?"

"Fine, just fine," Lesley grinned back. "As you can see," she said, indicating the table, "I only got up to eat."

"Nothing fancy," Cass shrugged. "It's just a pasta salad and some canned soup. I didn't want you to wake up and not find me here, so I decided against running out to the store."

They sat at the small circular table, and Cass said grace briefly.

"Do you usually go to church on Sundays?" Lesley asked, suddenly feeling guilty. "I hope I didn't mess up your schedule."

"Nah. I really only go when I'm at home. Or when my mother's visiting," Cass answered. "I'm a believer, but I'm not devout. When I was growing up in Antigua, my mother and grandmother took us to church every Sunday, which was OK. But I went to a convent school, and we had to go to Mass on the first Friday of each month, not to mention every other religious holiday. Easter! Forget it! My mother would dress us up and drag us to a three-hour church service on Good Friday. Can you imagine wearing a purple wool dress on a Friday afternoon in the tropics?"

Lesley laughed. "Purple wool?"

"My aunt lived in England and bought most of our clothes," Cass explained. "And only grownups could wear black. Kids wore white or purple. Anyway, I promised that when I grew up I'd never attend another Good Friday service. And I haven't!"

"I know exactly what you mean," Lesley said quietly. "I could tell you all about my church days, but that'd take a month or so."

The afternoon passed easily and soon, too soon, Lesley began to get herself together for the trip home. "It's Dow," she said to Cass's protests. "We always talk on Sundays, and he'll be worried if he calls and I'm not there."

"You're welcome to use my phone to call him," Cass offered quickly.

Lesley declined graciously. "That's so nice of you," she said, "but I really should go anyway."

At the door, she took Cass's number, jotting it down on the back of a dry-cleaning receipt from her purse, and hugged Cass briefly. "Thanks so much for a great time," she called as she stepped into the elevator. "I'll call you later, Cassandra."

"It's Cass!" Cass corrected her good-naturedly.

"Right! Cass."

Staring out the train window, Lesley smiled at the gathering darkness. We should have been friends in high school, she told herself. We have so much in common.

5

It was 6:00 o'clock on Sunday and Cass hadn't slept since Friday. She had fully intended to crash on the couch last night, but tiptoeing into the bedroom to get her things, she had found herself watching Lesley sleep, listening to the soft, rhythmic breathing, tracing the tall form outlined beneath the covers by the light spilling through the half-open door. And right then Cass had known she was lost.

Instead of going to bed, she had made herself a pot of lemon grass tea and sat in the early-morning darkness. "It's all my imagination," she'd scolded herself; "it'll pass. I'll probably feel different when she wakes up. She'll just be a girl I used to know back in high school who's now a woman that's lonely and hurting. Christ! I need a vacation!"

She resolved then to pay her parents a visit soon; to take a vacation maybe during the February break. Moving to the window and staring down at the city, she had deliberately absented herself, imagining the heat and sunshine of her island home, and forcing herself to forget the calm breathing in the bedroom down the hall.

Now Cass closed the door behind Lesley and leaned against it for a long time, unseeing, unthinking, even. Finally she sighed and went to clear the table. She had wanted Lesley to stay longer, and she was afraid that she had seemed too lonely, herself; too pushy, perhaps. She tried to examine her motives, if there were any. The woman had recently lost her husband; was she exploiting Lesley's weakness? No, she didn't think so. She hadn't found Lesley weak. She couldn't love a weak woman, anyway.

Cass pulled herself up. As her mother would have said, she was running quite ahead of herself. Suppose the woman didn't even call. She promised herself that if Lesley *did* call, she would take control of her feelings and they would simply be friends. But she deluded herself, she knew. This warm, intelligent, sensitive and ¾ oh, God! ¾ beautiful woman was one she wanted to love, one she could stay with for the long haul. She didn't wonder how she knew; she knew, that was all.

Moving swiftly now so that she could watch *60 Minutes*, Cass took a shower, washed her hair and donned a nightshirt. Going through the dry cleaning still hanging on the closet door, she selected a suit for the next day. She had to be at work for 8:45, but she liked to get in early.

Throwing her briefcase onto the bed, she attempted to organize the literature she'd picked up at the conference while she watched Ed Bradley. "Man, if I were straight," she mused, as usual. The show was interesting, but her eyes were gritty with sleep; she wouldn't make it to Andy Rooney tonight.

She was in a deep sleep when the phone rang.

"Cassandra?" came the questioning voice.

"No," she responded, immediately awake, "it's Cass."

"Right, right," Lesley laughed. "Well, I got home safely. *Obviously*. I spoke to the boys and got myself ready for work tomorrow and now I'm in bed."

Don't do this to me, Cass groaned to herself; I remember what you look like in bed.

"Well, I'm glad to hear you made it home safely," she said instead, suddenly feeling shy. "It was really great seeing you. ...."

"Yeah, you, too. Go back to sleep. I'll call you tomorrow night to make arrangements to meet after work, OK."

"That's fine," was all Cass could manage.

"Well, good night, then," Lesley murmured, "and thanks, again."

"'Night."

Cass laughed aloud and hugged her pillow. "I'll take it any way I can get it," she said. She dragged the blanket over her, imagining she could detect Lesley's scent on it as she did so.

6

Early Tuesday evening, Cass took Lesley to Tío Pépé, her favorite Mexican restaurant, in Greenwich Village. The place wasn't crowded, but Cass requested a table in the back so they could enjoy some privacy. Laughing and talking, they shared seafood paella and washed it down with a pitcher of sangria. Cass was at her entertaining best and there was no doubt that Lesley was having a good time.

As the friendship flourished, increasingly Lesley began to take the Long Island Railroad to work, meeting Cass at her subway stop at the end of the day. It was a welcome and even necessary change, since her car was getting to be more trouble than she cared to handle. She had been driving the same vehicle since her boys were in high school, and on cold mornings the old station wagon was hard to start. It wasn't much longer, therefore, before Lesley began to bring an overnight bag and take the train into Brooklyn with Cass.

At the end of their day, back at Cass's apartment, they would often share West Indian takeout while they took care of their paperwork. At other times they would go out to eat at Carmine's, then take in a movie. They both loved movies and in the city Lesley got to enjoy films that normally wouldn't have played on the Island. On occasion, they would take advantage of the good weather and walk all the way down to 57th Street where they would browse for hours in Coliseum Books. Lesley loved the liveliness of the city and reveled in its freedoms.

Cass never ventured out to Lesley's house, however. She claimed the Island was too far, too quiet, too suburban for her. In truth, she did not want to be in the house that Lesley had shared with her husband, knowing she would feel like an interloper. She jokingly disparaged suburbia and always proposed something to do in Manhattan instead.

Fall was Lesley's favorite time of year and her pleasure in the changing colors gradually infected Cass, the Caribbean devotee who craved sunlight and greenery. They took to strolling in Central Park before the early darkness fell. Cass loved walking a few paces behind Lesley, watching as she would deliberately kick through mounds of fallen leaves.

18

Sometimes Lesley would swing around, a wide smile lighting her face as she pointed out some reddish-orange swath of leaves that caught her eye.

"God, I *love* this woman," Cass would groan inwardly.

The first morning that they came downstairs and could see their breath curl up in little puffs, Lesley laughed with delight. "Look," she said, pursing her lips and blowing out little curlicues. Before Cass knew it, she, too, had joined in the game, abandoning her low-key morning persona to mouth ethereal shapes.

This week, they were talking about an excursion to either Westchester or New Jersey to find Lesley a new car. Gene had chosen the vehicle she currently drove, as he did all their major purchases, and Lesley was looking forward to getting what she wanted for a change. So she and Cass spent a great deal of time car-watching in the crowded city and poring over automobile magazines.

Their steadily deepening friendship filled a need in both women. Neither had fully experienced that subtle teenage passage, that gritty initiation into womanhood when girls learn to negotiate the sometimes slippery roads of female friendships. Neither had enjoyed the euphoria of sleepovers, shopping expeditions, mutual forays into the wonders of makeup, or pubescent sexual explorations ¾ the glory and the pain of adolescence.

Lesley had an older sister, Lana, but they had not been particularly close growing up, and the distance that separated them now was more than physical. While their mother had been a good caretaker, she had not been a warm parent; she reserved her love for her husband and her devotion for her church, around which their family life revolved.

Lesley had been a member of many of the church's groups and activities; but she felt confined by, rather than close to, the daughters of the congregation which behaved as though Judgment Day was imminent. Lana felt the same constriction and, in her struggle to be free, distanced herself even from her sister.

Cass, on the other hand, had always been the object of her family's love and attention by virtue of being the only daughter and the youngest child. Her mother was indulgent and her father and brothers protective. However, Cass had been uprooted from her home at 14, and her tenuous school friendships had not survived; neither had they been replaced after her disastrous introduction to high school in New York.

Understandably, to the two women every outing became an event, every overnight an exercise in bonding. Had they been the same size, no doubt they would have traded shoes and clothes like teenagers. Clowning and acting silly, gorging themselves late at night, or giggling on the phone, it never occured to either of them to admonish the other to grow up. They had been grown far too early and too long, and they were enjoying the experience of reclaiming the lost in-between.

Naturally, every day was not a party. Occasionally, Lesley would lapse into periods of silence and Sunday afternoon departures would envelop her in gloom. Fearful that Lesley was depressed by memories of her husband, Cass would make her heavily sweetened cups of lemon grass tea, which she loved, and do her best Diana Ross and the Supremes imitations until Lesley laughed again. When she couldn't jolly Lesley out of her moods, Cass would join in, sitting on the floor next to Lesley's chair and hanging her face gravely, like a mutt abandoned at a shelter, until they would both burst into laughter.

Thanksgiving's approach found Lesley under a cloud, and, try as she would, Cass could not dissipate it. Lesley smiled at Cass's clowning, but the light never reached her eyes, and although she seemed unhappy at the apartment, she expressed no desire to go home.

"Shit, Lesley!" Cass finally exploded. "There's a holiday weekend coming up and you're dragging around the place like the shadow of death! What the hell is wrong with you, anyway?"

To her shock and amazement, Lesley crumpled onto the couch in tears.

"Oh, God! What happen'? What?" Cass's speech became markedly Caribbean, as it always did during moments of stress. "Sorry," she groaned, ignorant of what she had done, but blaming herself nonetheless. "I'm sorry."

She held her friend's body and rocked her back and forth, instinctively adopting her mother's comfort mode and crooning wordless sounds of sympathy. When the tears stopped, she used the tail of her shirt to dry Lesley's face, then pinched her nose. "Blow," she said, smiling.

Lesley smiled, in turn, and shook her head.

"I'm sorry," she said. "It's just that ¾ you know ¾ what you said about it being Thanksgiving and all. It was Gene's favorite holiday ...

20

and I'm not looking forward to it without him. Generes didn't come home last year, so me and the boys went to my parents and it was awful! Just awful!" Her eyes filled up again.

"But you can stay here, Lesley," Cass burst out. "You know that."

"But what about your family? Your brother in Westchester? And the one in Connecticut? Won't they be expecting you?"

"Well, I usually go to Marcus and Sylvie's, but I saw them both over Labor Day, so they'll understand. ... Tell you what: You spend Thanksgiving weekend with me, and I'll make dinner. Not turkey, though," she warned. "I'll make something West Indian. Potato dumplings with all the trimmings, how's that?" she cajoled. "Hmm, how's that?"

"But what about the boys?" Lesley was plaintive. "They'll expect to come home for dinner."

"Boys? Boys! Girl, you need to tell those hardback men to give you a break! They must have girlfriends or someplace else they can eat."

The decision having been taken out of her hands, Lesley went along with the plan. After work that Wednesday, she and Cass went to the bodegas on Flatbush Avenue and shopped for their West Indian Thanksgiving.

Indefinably, each felt that a change had entered their relationship.

7

Moving around each other like seasoned professionals, Cass cooked the meal while Lesley made apple and Key lime pies for dessert. The silence was easy and the aroma of good food permeated the apartment.

Lesley's sons called separately in the early afternoon. After speaking to his mother, Seth spoke briefly to Cass, wishing her Happy Thanksgiving and thanking her for having his mother. Cass was both touched and wryly amused. She smiled privately. If you only knew, she thought.

They had decided to dress up for the occasion. Cass wore navy dress slacks and a light blue broadcloth shirt, while Lesley sported a short, maroon silk dress that Cass had persuaded her to buy; it showed off her legs and complemented the maroon and gray paisley slippers they had picked up in a little shop on 57th Street. She borrowed Cass's signature scent, Blue Grass, and spritzed both of them. Posturing in front of the mirror, they complimented each other, then took pictures with Cass's old Polaroid.

Lesley's gaiety seemed a trifle forced and Cass suspected she had cried in the shower. A surge of annoyance went through Cass, followed quickly by a feeling of shame. It was only natural, after all, that Lesley should feel a bit nostalgic at this time, she chided herself.

Linking hands, they each offered a short grace, blessing their families, the homeless and each other. The food was good and they indulged in several helpings, each making an effort to keep the mood celebratory. They praised the merits of Caribbean and Southern cooking and compared holiday traditions. After washing the dishes and tidying the kitchen, they retreated to the living room to rest their stuffed bodies on the couch, still chatting about family holidays.

"Did you speak to your brothers today, Cass?" Lesley asked. "I didn't hear you call."

"I spoke to them on Tuesday night," Cass answered. "I told them I would be going out of town so that they wouldn't bother calling."

"You know, we were so busy with the cooking and everything else, I hardly noticed, but that phone hasn't rung for you all day. Don't tell me I'm your only friend," Lesley said with a laugh.

She lay across two of the seat cushions, legs crossed and draped over the arm of the couch, causing the hem of her dress to fall back suggestively.

Seated in the corner next to Lesley's head, Cass fought the urge to run her hands through the hair that strayed onto her lap.

"You're the only friend I want," Cass answered, her voice suddenly deep.

Sensing that things had suddenly turned serious, Lesley swung her legs around and sat up, facing Cass. "What?" she asked, her eyes narrowing. "What do you mean?"

"You know."

"I know?" Lesley queried weakly, her heart suddenly racing. "Know what?"

Cass stared at her.

"Look at me," she invited softly. "You know what I'm talking about. I'm in love with you, Lesley Gorton. I love you ... like a woman loves a woman"

Lesley covered her face in confusion, and Cass peeled her hands away, gripping them tightly. "Look at me. *I said, look at me!*" She spoke fiercely and clearly, mouthing the words carefully. "Hardly anyone calls when you're here, because, usually, I turn the phone off, OK. I don't want *anybody* intruding on us, on the time we spend together. I've already got Gene to compete with."

Lesley wrested her hands away and began to cry.

"I love every moment I spend with you, and I hate every moment you spend in Westbury, OK. I want to be with you," Cass continued urgently, her words picking up speed. "I want to take care of you. You don't have to stay in that empty house on Long Island with your memories. There's a hundred other Thanksgivings coming and a hundred Christmases and two hundred birthdays, and I want to spend them with you."

She moved closer and Lesley retreated. "What?" Cass asked, pained. "You're afraid of me now? Why? What have I ever done to you but love you?"

But her love lay like a ditch between them, and she searched Lesley's face looking for a way to cross over. All she read there was confusion mixed with embarrassment and some vague, misunderstood sense of betrayal.

Watching her in silence for a few moments, Cass felt old, weary. "You want to leave? Don't you? *Don't you?* Then go."

Wiping her face with the backs of her hands, Lesley stumbled down the hall to the bedroom and picked up her purse. She returned to the living room where Cass stood, staring out the window. Unsure of what to say, Lesley whispered, "Thanks for dinner."

"The pleasure was mine," Cass replied coldly. "And, obviously, only mine."

She didn't turn around.

8

Getting a cab was easy. Everyone had gone away for Thanksgiving, it seemed, because the streets were virtually deserted. Lesley fought to control her sobbing in the car. She felt frightened, betrayed. Everything had been going so well; were the past two months a lie? Why did Cass have to do this to her? Tricking her, pretending to be her friend when all she wanted to do was hit on her. Just like that jerk of a doctor at the Veterans Hospital, pretending to console her after Gene died.

You just never knew people, did you? Who would have thought Cass was that type? Now she had lost two friends in one year.

There was no immediate train because of the holiday schedule. Settling down to wait, Lesley noticed an obviously deranged man staring at her as though *she* were crazy. Hoping he would leave her alone, she looked down, and understood the reason for his stare. She was still dressed for indoors, in her thin slip dress and *peau de soie* mules. She carried no coat, not even a jacket. Briefly, she worried that he might think she was a hooker. What was really surprising, she thought, was that she had not even felt the cold. Luckily, the station was warm, as the train would be. She only had to worry about the dash to her car in the railroad's parking lot.

She delayed thinking about the scene at Cass's apartment, deliberately pushing it from her every time it intruded. She got up and purchased a magazine, leafing through it but seeing nothing.

The train, when it came, was also practically empty. There was no one across from her to study; in the darkness outside, nothing to see. Cass's face came back to her, full of pain. She had not meant to hurt Cass's feelings; she had backed away instinctively, retreating from a situation she had absolutely no idea how to handle.

"How could you *not* have known?" she berated herself. "Only an idiot wouldn't have had a clue ...

"But how *could* I have known?" she countered. "She looked ordinary. Attractive, yes, but just like anybody else.

25

"Come on, Lesley," she chided. "Now you're trafficking in stereotypes. What does gay look like? What did you expect? A crewcut, jeans and Army boots? Tattoos and grease under her fingernails? You're supposed to be smarter than that.

"Didn't you wonder why she didn't have a boyfriend, had never been married?

"No, a lot of straight women never marry, and some don't have boyfriends either," she told herself defensively. "I don't!

"And there you were, having a gay old time. Oops, a *grand* old time. You loved being there, didn't you, dancing, eating, sleeping over. Wonder how many women she's had in that bed...

"Well, if she fell in love with me, was I doing something to encourage it. I wonder if I have those tendencies, too. My God! What were people thinking about us? Good thing my kids hadn't met her...

"Admit it. You must have felt some currents. *Something*.

"Well, yes, but not until earlier this week, and even then, I wasn't sure what it was. How could I be? I never knew any gay people before. Well, come to think of it, I must have. But I just didn't know they were gay!"

She tormented herself into Westbury, through the parking lot and into her car. As the old station wagon struggled to warm up, she asked herself: "Why did she do it? And why didn't I see?" She replayed the scene over and over in her mind. The deepening voice as Cass said, *You're the only friend I want.* The earnestness in her light eyes, the emotion choking her, the pain wrapped in anger as Lesley backed away.

Turning the wheezing car into her driveway, Lesley noticed that both her neighbors had holiday company. Lights were blazing and voices were raised in camaraderie. And loneliness loomed up like a force field before her.

You're the only friend I want. Entering the house, she suddenly felt the cold.

9

It seemed to Cass that she stood at the window for hours. Finally, moving like an automaton, she began to get ready for bed. Meticulously she hung her clothes to air on the curtain rod in the bathroom, cleaned her face with Pond's, and brushed her teeth. Staring into the mirror, all she could see was Lesley's face as she retreated from her. She put the television on and got into bed. Lesley's face still stared at her from the screen. She wasn't sure if *Seinfeld* would be on tonight, but she would keep the set on for company, anyway.

Cass had had relationships end before; hell, she generally ended them herself. She had known some lovely women; smart women who were going places in their careers; women who wanted to settle down and build a long-term relationship. She'd even been in love once. During graduate school she had had a wonderful two-year relationship with a young teacher¾had even considered moving to Boston when the woman accepted a position there.

Why had she done it? Why was it that she *had* to tell Lesley? She could have had months and months with her before this came up. But how do you prepare someone for something like this, anyway, she wondered. And why *shouldn't* she tell her? How much longer could she have continued this charade? How many more weekends could she have spent listening to Lesley's stories of Gene, without declaring, "I *know* how Gene felt about you, Lesley. I know perfectly well, because I feel the same way."

Unqualifiedly, this was the worst night of her life. When her family had left the West Indies, at least there had been the excitement of America to temper the pain. She understood, now, how lonely people became overweight, because she was tempted to go back to the kitchen and finish the apple pie. There was this horrible, awful emptiness in her gut.

Lesley was probably on the train now, she brooded. Most likely shuddering with relief at her narrow escape. Cass wondered why on earth she had fallen for a straight woman. It was probably to test her liberal views on love. She'd always been aggressively supportive of

27

friends who crossed the color or the ethnic line, or who broke age barriers and marriage vows in order to find that elusive emotion. Maybe if she had told them to stick to their own kind, their own group, she wouldn't be in this predicament now.

It was her mother's fault, of course. Often despite the evidence to the contrary, Roma Shortman had led her daughter to believe that love could overcome anything. Cass recalled the day she had celebrated her second master's degree; the day she had come out to her mother. After all the family and friends were gone, Roma had come upstairs to Cass's old room and lain across the bed. She had looked at her daughter, pride and love making her eyes shine behind her glasses.

"So," she had asked Cass, "what's next?" Years spent in London and New York had diluted but not eradicated her Antiguan accent. "You've got your education. What now? What about *you*? You can't go to sleep with a piece of paper come nighttime, you know," she'd said gently. "I want to see you settled down, C'sandra. You don't have a soul to bring a cup of water for you if anything should happen to us, and me and your father are getting old now. I know your brothers are not going to see you want for anything, but they have their wives, after all ... So tell me what you're going to do."

Cass looked at her mother's carefully pressed and styled hair, and she was amazed to see how the gray was proliferating. Although her body was still sturdy, her mother favored her left foot, which was forever swollen after more than 30 years on duty.

This was the woman who, despite three close and difficult pregnancies, had tried yet again for a girl. Since she had succeeded, she had spent the rest of her days making sure her only daughter knew that she was loved and wanted. In the first two years of her life, Cass had spent more time in her mother's arms than had her three brothers all together. In fact, her grandmother used to say it was a wonder that Cass had ever learned to walk.

To lie to Roma now would be to shortchange that love. Her expectations were reasonable; her questions justified.

"Mother," Cass said, rising from the bed and sitting on the old trunk that served as a window seat. She wanted to look her mother straight in the eye when she told her. "You know what a lesbian is?"

Roma Shortman just stared. Then, slowly, "Girl, you trying to tell me you're *funny?*" She was a nurse; of course she knew the correct term. She simply could not bring herself to use it; not to her own daughter, no.

Cass nodded.

Roma looked puzzled. She still stared, but Cass knew she was not seeing her. As if she could read her mother's thoughts, she saw Roma retracing the past 30 years, wondering if it was something she had done, something she had neglected to do:

"Is it because she didn't have a sister; spent all that time with her brothers? I *did* warn them not to play so rough with her, to remember she was a little girl. And her father said she was all right. Or maybe it's because I didn't allow her to have boyfriends in school. That must be it! I should have encouraged her to invite boys over; allowed her to learn how to deal with boys other than her brothers. But then, with my schedule, who was here to supervise them?"

She turned things over and over in her mind, and still they did not add up.

"When she was small, she loved pretty things. She had nice dresses. She loved dolls.... I don't understand how this happened."

Roma finally spoke aloud. "Since when?"

"Mother, I knew even before we left home," Cass answered with care. "I've always known. Why'd you think I never went to Washington to visit James, way back then?"

She stopped, looked at the face before her pinched with pain. Her mother seemed to be taking it badly and Cass was stricken with guilt. "I know you had high hopes for me, and believe me, Mother, I'm sorry. Sorry to be such a disappointment to you."

There was a long silence, a long, long silence, and Cass grew afraid. Had she expected too much of her mother? Pushed her too far with this admission? Suppose she told her to take her things and leave? For good. She shivered suddenly, though it was not cold.

Mrs. Shortman walked to the other window and leaned against the glass, gazing down at the apple tree whose fruit no one would eat. Finally, she turned around and came toward her child.

"I wanted to see you married, of course, C'sandra. All this stuff," she indicated the house, in general, "everything I bought, everything I made ¾ I was saving for you. And your children."

There were tears in her eyes, and Cass looked away.

"Every day I see women who want children lose them over and over. And every day, I nurse babies for women who don't want them at all: crippled-up children, retarded children, children sick from drugs. Me? I was lucky. I wanted my children, and every one of you-all was born healthy. I wanted a girl, and the Lord gave me a girl. ...

"Boys leave their mother when they get married, you know," she said wryly, "but daughters, daughters are forever."

She touched her daughter's face lightly and the tears fell then. "Look at you ¾ how you're pretty. And so bright. And honest, too. A disappointment, C'sandra? I couldn't fly in God's face," she said staunchly.

Her lips trembling, Cassandra jumped up from the trunk, clutched her mother and bawled. Roma was still the mother she knew: her first line of defense, fiercely loyal, immutable, still standing upright where the average person would have stumbled.

When she could speak again, Cassandra released her mother and sat on the bed. "You want me to tell Daddy tonight?" she inquired.

"No," her mother said, rubbing Cass's back reassuringly, "I will take care of it."

On her next visit home, Cass's father had invited her for ice-cream, his age-old way of initiating a private conversation with his wife or one of his children. Sometimes he actually even bought them a cone.

Drury Shortman had been direct. "Your mother is worried that you haven't settled down by now. And she's afraid you're going to end up by yourself, Fish," he said, calling her by her old nickname. Cass adored him; he still treated her like she was 14 years old and new to America.

"To tell you the truth," he continued, "I'm concerned too. We're not getting any younger, after all, and you don't have anybody to provide for you, if anything should happen."

Keeping his eyes on the road, he frowned thoughtfully. He didn't understand young women these days. When Roma was Cass's age, they had been married for years already and had a family.

"You joined your pension plan?" he asked sharply. Cass nodded, wondering now what her mother had actually told him.

Then lowering his voice confidentially, her father continued, "We know you have to pay all your student loans and everything else, so we're going to leave the house at home for you, OK. You won't have to worry about a roof over your head, but make sure you save your money in case of sickness.

"Don't say anything," her father admonished, as though he expected some protest.

She nodded dumbly. Cass had not expected this at all. While she *had* thought of the future, she had never gone that far. She was 30 years old and had never worried about where she would live or what would happen if she got sick. But her security-conscious Caribbean parents obviously had, and as they had done all her life, they were looking out for their daughter.

Putting away the memories, Cass sighed. Maybe her parents had bred in her unreasonable expectations of the world. Anyway, the strain was over. At least she'd be able to get some real sleep now. She wouldn't have to lie alone on the sofabed, struggling for hours to forget that Lesley was sleeping down the hall. She would immerse herself in her work and her books, maybe even spend some weekends in Westchester with her brother's family and reacquaint herself with her much-neglected friends.

Contradicting her sense of relief, she got up and went into the bathroom for a slug of Nyquil. A cheap escape, it always put her out. As her thoughts began to cloud, she told herself that she was happy she had turned off the phone; that she didn't want Lesley calling her, disturbing her fragile sense of peace.

Not even to herself would Cass admit that it was easier to leave the phone disconnected than not hear it ring.

31

10

This was the longest, loneliest weekend of Lesley's life. Even when Gene had been mute with pain and even after the funeral, she had never been so lonely. This time there was no comforting face or voice to help her. In fact, there was not one soul to whom she could talk about what had happened, what she was going through.

The boys did not even call to distract her, since she had told them she was spending the holiday in the City. Sure, her parents lived only a short distance away, but what could she say to them? Under ordinary circumstances, she visited only from a sense of duty.

Lesley had never really forgiven her mother for her cold comfort on the day of Gene's funeral. Tired of trying to be strong for her own children's sake, she had turned to her mother, frightened and weeping. "Mama, he's gone," she had sobbed, laying her head on her mother's shoulder in a desperate search for comfort. "Mama, Gene is *gone....*"

Mrs. Hillary, forever on that rarefied spiritual plane on which only she could live, had taken Lesley by the shoulders and said to her firmly: "My dear, Jesus lives."

Immediately, Lesley's tears had stopped and she turned back to her kids. The effect might have been what she intended, but Mrs. Hillary would never know that in that specific moment Lesley rejected her. Finally, Lesley realized that her mother was utterly incapable of demonstrating the love of Jesus that she always professed, even toward her own daughter.

If there was anything to be said to her father's credit, it was that he was a good provider. But Dowson Hillary was a man's man and never seemed comfortable in his house, constantly filled with members of his wife's church. When he was home, he would be found in the garage in good weather, or in the basement if it was cold. Certainly, he perceived that there were emotional needs in his daughters, but he had no idea how to fill them. To compensate, he resorted to slipping them money when their mother was not looking.

Scratch her parents. Being extremely liberal, her daughter might have understood, but Generes lived in Florida and would not be home until Christmas. Though she could have spoken to her by phone, Lesley was not sure she was comfortable placing such a burden on her daughter. So she labored alone and longed for Monday when she could go back to work.

Even then, the week dragged.

Going straight home from Brooklyn felt strange, unfamiliar, isolating. She missed Cass and their routines ¾ the meals, the music, the shop talk ¾ the basic comfort she derived from being in Cass's company.

On Friday night, she was in bed before seven. She didn't bother to get out of pajamas on Saturday. On Sunday, she sat in her kitchen and questiond her motives for walking out. "I love you ... like a woman loves a woman," Cass had said.

Lesley had grown up surrounded by women. Her mother was a member of every women's group in her church, so Lesley and Lana had belonged, too, by extension. Yet the girls had never felt included. They hated the scrutiny they attracted simply by virtue of being their mother's daughters; the children of the fanatically religious Sister Hillary who played the church's organ, coached the choir and generally oversaw the youth groups.

From the time she was old enough to grate cheese, Lesley had been pressed into cooking service for every baptism, revival and wake. She cleaned the church and ironed choir robes every Saturday. She taught the children's class at Sunday school and served at the breakfast after morning service. And always, always, she was "Sister Hillary's little girl," but not one of them.

When she reached high school, her mother said Lesley was old enough to make her own declaration for Christ. Lesley declared she was quitting the choir and the Sunday school, and her mother said her soul was in her own hands.

Looking back, it seemed to Lesley that that was the first and last decision she had ever made. She had married straight out of high school ¾ she'd had to ¾ and remained in her parents' house for years, even after Gene had returned from Vietnam. Then there had been the kids.

Just before she met Cass, Lesley had begun slowly facing the realization that since her husband had died, her life had no focus, no purpose. She felt like a stripped tree, unable to provide fruit or shade. Her three children were grown and could fill their own needs. Her father had her mother, and her mother had God.

I love you like a woman loves a woman.

Cass had brought her out of the dark tunnel of depression that had started with Gene's diagnosis. She had helped her overcome her unacknowledged feelings of abandonment by Gene's friends. Over the past months, she had chuckled, giggled, sometimes laughed uproariously. She had sung calypso choruses aloud. Cass had given her back an appetite and the gift of sleep ¾nightlong, deep, refreshing sleep.

Cass had shown her unconditional acceptance, which had translated into a wonderful sense of security. She had never broken even a casual promise. Cass had made her feel at home; she had narrowed her own life in order to expand Lesley's.

I love you like a woman loves a woman.

So that was what it felt like. Why, then, had she run away? Wasn't this what she had been searching for all her life? If she had found all this in a man, wouldn't she have stayed?

On Monday, Lesley began to wonder, "Can I go back? Would she *have* me back?" Then: "Why *should* she have me back?"

By Tuesday morning, she had exhausted herself with her thoughts, and as she sat in her car and listened to its harsh cough, she closed her eyes in despair. She called in sick, took a couple of sleeping pills and returned to bed. She was running away again, she knew, but she didn't care.

That evening, as she pacified herself by eating macaroons in bed, she decided to watch the 5:00 o'clock news. She listened, horrified, to reports of the tragic incident that had taken place: someone had opened fire in a railroad car during rush hour. Ordinarily she would have been home from work already at that time, yet Lesley trembled at the fatal madness that had occured at the Garden City station.

The phone rang and she grabbed it immediately.

"Hello," she said, warily.

It was Ginny, calling in response to the news report. Reassuring her that she was safe, though shaken, Lesley impulsively invited Ginny to meet her for dinner. It would be good to get out of herself for a while, she thought, as she coaxed the old car into life and headed out into the cold darkness.

The food was mediocre, but the diner was already cheerily decorated for Christmas. It was wonderful to see Ginny, always her favorite among the old group. They talked of the times they had shared, of golfing bets they'd won and lost, and of Christmas trips to the City to shop and take in a show. Lesley was surprised to find that she could talk about Gene without choking up, without the customary aching sense of loss. Instead she felt a sense of pleasure, a certain satisfaction that they had enjoyed many good years and that he was remembered by the others so fondly.

Over dessert, Ginny inquired how Lesley's kids were doing and Lesley felt confident enough to ask her, for the first time, why she and Leroy had never had children.

Gazing straight into Lesley's eyes, Ginny replied in her soft Arkansas drawl, "Because we couldn't."

Lesley's face burned. "I'm sorry," she said. Sorry that she had asked and sorry for Ginny.

As though she had read her thoughts, Ginny said straightforwardly, "There was nothing wrong with me; it was Leroy. I wanted to adopt, but he didn't. He had four brothers and four sisters, all with a bunch of kids, and it was humiliating for him not to be able to have any of his own. So all these years he's just said he had enough nieces and nephews and didn't want any kids. I think he even believes it now." She smiled.

"I love kids and I believe I would have made a good mother ¾ but it just wasn't meant to be." She shrugged. "You never get things exactly the way you want them in life, Les, but I've gotten used to it. And, you know, Leroy might not have been able to give me kids, but there was nothing he *could* give me that I didn't get."

As she drove home, Lesley mulled over Ginny's words. Pulling into the driveway, she sighed; she had forgotten to leave the lights on and the dark house looked cold, uninviting.

You don't have to stay in that empty house on Long Island with your memories. We can make new ones together.

Abruptly, she backed out of the driveway and headed for the railroad station. Drawing in a deep breath, she ran to the ticket window and purchased a fare to the City.

11

Cass was frantic now. She didn't care if she lost face; she just *had* to know that Lesley was OK. From the minute she had heard of the massacre on the railroad, she had begun to sweat. Was Lesley on that train? Was she? She told herself that Lesley, even if she had taken the train today, would have been home long before the incident. But suppose she'd had to stop some place? Suppose she had worked late? Cass couldn't stop torturing herself.

Finally, she resolved to find out for sure. If Lesley answered the phone, she promised herself, she would simply hang up. That's all she needed to know, anyway: that she was home, safe, alive.

Cass had turned her phone back on a couple days after Lesley's departure. When it did not ring, she'd told herself that Lesley had probably given up calling after not getting an answer. Now she felt what it was like to be on the other end of the line, as Lesley's phone rang and rang and rang. She hung up and called repeatedly. Nobody who was at home would be able to stand that racket, she thought; Lesley would have to answer the phone. But for hours, there was no answer.

Who to call? Cass, for the first time, realized just how insulated their association had been. Their whole relationship had been conducted in a cocoon. Neither knew the friends of the other; outside of work, they had no one in common. If Lesley wasn't home by 9:00 o'clock, Cass decided, she would call Mrs. Hillary.

At 9:00, she dialed information and got Mrs. Hillary's number. She was not at home. And Seth and Dow were unlisted.

"Fuck!" she exploded in a rare expletive.

Getting emotional always made her ravenous. She would order in some food and then call Lesley's house once more after she had eaten.

Forcing herself to sit, she waited for the delivery. The apathy she had worn for the past two weeks had fallen away. Now she acknowledged that she missed Lesley ¾ achingly. She had read books, rented movies, indulged in several "unscheduled" calls to her mother and her

brother at home. And still, she had felt that ache ¾ like a hunger long
unsatisfied.

She recalled some lines from a poem she had learned as a girl:

I cried for madder music and for stronger wine,
But when the feast is finished and the lamps expire,
Then falls thy shadow, Cynara! the night is thine,
And I am desolate and sick of an old passion,
Yea hungry for the lips of my desire:
I have been faithful to thee, Cynara! in my fashion.

As young as she had been, she had been moved by the pain and
passion in those words, and she had longed to love someone like that.
She smiled now at her foolishness.

The bell rang. "That was fast," she muttered.

She looked through the peephole before she opened the door, and
her eyes widened as they took in Lesley standing on the threshold.

"How did you get here?" Cass blurted stupidly, as she moved aside
to let her pass.

"The train."

Cass leaned against the door, weak with relief of all sorts. Lesley
was alive; she was here, standing in all her earthy beauty in Cass's own
living room. Again. She raised her palms in a questioning gesture and
then let them fall slowly. "So you're all right then? I thought you might
have been on that train ... ." Her words trailed away.

Lesley shook her head. "No, I didn't even go in today."

"Why? Were you sick?"

"In a manner of speaking, yes."

"You all right now?"

"I guess."

They stood awkwardly for a minute, and the silence bloomed with
questions.

"I missed you," Lesley said simply.

"I missed you, too," Cass answered. "I'm glad you came back."

"I didn't think you'd have me back," Lesley admitted. "I thought
..."

The bell rang again. This time it was the food. As if there had been

37

no break in their routine, the women set the little table, plugged in the kettle and took plates down from the cupboard. Cass heaped the plates with fried rice and scallops in garlic sauce, while Lesley poured lemon tea into the big pottery mugs that said "Antigua." She sighed as she sat down.

"I ate less than two hours ago, and I'm still hungry," Lesley commented.

"You went out to eat with someone," Cass said, slightly accusing.

"Yeah, I met Ginny for dinner. How'd you know?"

"I called your house and there was no answer for hours," Cass explained. She told Lesley how worried ¾ frantic ¾she had been when she heard of the shooting on the train. How she had even resorted to calling Mrs. Hillary.

Lesley, in turn, confessed to Cass how terribly empty the past two weeks had been. Haltingly, she told her about the demons she had wrestled; shared with her the conclusions she had finally reached.

"I know that you love me," she said quietly, "and I'm happy that you do, but ..." She paused for a moment. "I guess what I'm trying to say is ¾ I'm not really sure how to love you, Cass. I don't know how to love a woman. I don't know what to do."

"You love me the way you would love a man, I would imagine," Cass answered gently. "In fact, it should be *easier* to love a woman. There's no need to play the games that men ..."

Lesley cut in: "But that's exactly it! I *know* those games. I know what to expect, what to do." She looked away with a frown.

"Look at me," Cass whispered, coming around the table and squatting before her. "It's the sex you're worried about, isn't it?"

Her eyes sliding away, Lesley nodded.

"I'm not going to *force* you to sleep with me, Lesley," Cass said. "This isn't simply about sex. I'm 43 years old and I know what I want: I want you with me. For good. I don't play games, and I don't make empty promises. I love you and I'll do everything I can honestly do to make you happy. I'm not going anywhere, so you take your time and let me know when you're ready, OK. In the meantime, I'll show you my AIDS tests if that'll make you more comfortable."

"I'm clean," Lesley reassured her. "I changed my insurance after Gene died, and I had to take the test. You know I haven't been with anyone, Cass ...."

"Good." Cass was relieved. She hadn't known how she would raise the subject if the time ever came, but this had been easy. Her respite was short, however.

"How am I going to tell my family, Cass?" Lesley asked abruptly. Cass thought a moment about her own father and wondered why she'd never had the courage to broach the subject with him. She exhaled slowly. "I don't know how," she admitted, "other than telling them together. And soon. The longer you leave it, the harder it becomes."

They talked until long past midnight, until they were emotionally and physically exhausted. Deciding they would both call in sick next day, Lesley went off to bed, while Cass made up the sofa.

Just before dawn, Cass felt a brief chill as the comforter was lifted. Without opening her eyes or turning, she shifted to accommodate Lesley behind her.

"I love you," Lesley whispered.

"I know."

As they settled themselves, the slight convexity of Lesley's stomach nestled into the concavity of Cass's lower back. The fit was perfect.

12

They resumed the car search. Lesley considered the car a Christmas present to herself and didn't want the new year to find her still looking.

On Saturday, they took Metro-North up to Tarrytown, where they were met by Cass's middle brother Marcus, a big, handsome man. Cass introduced Lesley as a friend from high school. Marcus did not remember her, but expressed pleasure at knowing her now. Displaying his own gap-toothed smile, he invited her to sit up front with him, relegating Cass to the back seat, which she took good-naturedly.

At the dealer, Lesley quickly decided on a Volkswagen Passat.

"Yep," she said, after driving the test, "this is what I want. It's easy to handle, it's solid and it's attractive. They're good cars. My friend Ginny's had a Jetta for years."

"But you haven't tried anything else," Marcus protested.

"Yes, we have," Cass interjected. "We've already been to New Jersey and Queens. I like this one, too."

Back at the showroom, Marcus sat down alongside Lesley to talk with the salesman. Cass didn't know who disgusted her more, the salesman who automatically assumed Lesley was Marcus's wife or Marcus, himself, who couldn't keep his eyes off Lesley. Thrusting her hands deep into her pockets, Cass walked outside, almost wishing she had not given up her Dunhills. But the sunshine was deceptive and the cold chased her back in.

The salesman, gratified that things had gone so easily, promised that everything would be ready by the following weekend, provided that her check cleared. Lesley had surprised him ¾ and Marcus ¾ by declaring she needed no financing. She wrote a personal check.

"Gene's insurance," she whispered to Cass. "I've been keeping it for something significant."

To celebrate, Marcus offered to treat them to an early dinner. Sliding into the booth next to Lesley, he faced Cass across the table. Turning on all his charm, he regaled them with stories about his job as an

40

administrator at Albert Einstein Hospital, turning ever so often to smile or direct a comment at Lesley.

Cass noticed that Lesley was quieter than usual and could not help wondering if she were simply self-conscious because of the attention, or regretful she hadn't met someone like Marcus first.

Feeling stupid, feeling confused, Cass excused herself and went to the bathroom. "I can't believe I'm feeling threatened by my own brother," she whispered to her reflection in the mirror. "Why would I think he's more attractive to her? Because he's male and I'm not?" She looked at herself objectively. "He has nothing on me. Same face, same smile. He's personable, and I'm personable, too. But what makes *me* more attractive," she told herself with determination, "is that *he* wants to fool around with her and I, *I love her.*"

Striding back to the table, she sat down and looked pointedly at her watch. "We have to be going, Bro," she announced.

"Already? No dessert, ladies? I guess you're watching your figures." Marcus smiled, looking pointedly at Lesley. "Well, it's been great having your company," he said, reaching inside his jacket. He placed a business card on the table in front of her. "If you have any questions about the car ..."

"If there are any questions," Cass said decisively, *"I'll* call you." She pushed the card back toward her brother.

One raised eyebrow acknowledged that he had gotten the message.

To his credit, Marcus coolly kept up the conversation on the drive back to the station. Cass sat in front, this time, and talked with him warmly, without rancor. When they parted, she threw her arms around him. "Bye, Bro," she smiled. "Give Sylvie and the kids my love."

Laughing, he hugged her back. "I'll do that, *Fish.*"

Lesley shook his hand and politely thanked him for his time and for dinner.

"Why were you so quiet back there?" Cass demanded, as soon as Marcus left. "Did he embarrass you?"

"No, not really. He was just being nice."

"Sure," Cass said sarcastically. "The man was hitting on you, Lesley. You don't have to pretend for me. I *know* my brother."

Lesley shrugged.

"Did you find him attractive?" Cass persisted.

"Yes, but not in the way you mean."

"How do I mean?"

"Well, Ray Charles could see that he's an attractive man," Lesley replied defensively. "I expected that. I've seen his pictures, remember?"

"But you weren't attracted to him?"

"He's *your brother!* Which would make him what, Cass? Technically my brother-in-law; am I right?" For the first time Cass realized that Lesley was angry. "Why did you do that with the card, huh? Why? Did you think I would call him the first chance I got? Are you going to trust me? Or are you going to interrogate me every time I talk to a man?"

Cass felt chastened. "I'm sorry; I'm sorry," she said. She tried to make a joke of it. "I've never been with a straight woman before, and I guess I don't know the protocol."

The joke didn't work; Lesley only glared

"I was trying to send a message to Marcus, that's all," Cass admitted. "I didn't mean to imply that I don't trust you."

There was silence for a few minutes before Lesley relented.

"It's OK. Forget it! Why did he call you Fish?"

"Revenge. It's a family name; but he knows I don't like being called 'Fish' in public."

"I'm not the public," Lesley countered. "How come you never told me?"

"I never told anyone."

"What does it mean anyway?"

"When I was little," Cass explained, "everyone doted on me because I was the only girl in the family, and one day my granny said that I was rotten ¾ like a spoiled fish. She called me 'Spoiled Fish' so often, the name just stuck, and it eventually became just 'Fish.'"

"So that explains the collection of fish in your apartment.," Lesley said. "I think it's a great story. How come you don't want anyone to know?"

"Please! *A lesbian named Fish?* What do you think I am ¾ a masochist?"

The following Sunday, Marcus picked them up and drove them to the dealership. He was a model of politeness and courtesy and even invited them back to the house. But they declined, citing the early darkness and their unfamiliarity with the roads.

Jotting down his directions, they thanked him again for his help, then raced back to Manhattan in Lesley's brand new Passat. The car ate up the miles, inspiring Cass to sing Tracy Chapman's "Fast Car" at the top of her lungs.

In this mood, Lesley got Cass to agree to spend Christmas at her house. Her kids would be home for the holiday, she said, and it was time for Cass to meet them and see the other part of her life.

Cass could muster no objection. They agreed to take a midday train on Christmas Eve so they could avoid the rush-hour crush.

13

Lesley was coming into the City today and Cass planned to meet her at Macy's. They would make their last-minute purchases then go back to the apartment to trim the tree. It was cold, cold, cold and Cass had been tempted to call and suggest they put off the shopping.

But when Lesley finally arrived, the weather became irrelevant. She was wearing a fitted wool coat in bright red, with black fur around the collar and cuffs. Her gloves and rolled brim hat were black with a red passamenterie design, and she sported black ankle boots. She also wore a million-watt smile.

To Cass she looked like she'd stepped straight out of a Currier & Ives greeting card, and she smacked her almost-numb lips in appreciation.

"Lady, where's your muff?" she inquired gaily.

"In my drawers, where it always is," Lesley quipped, with a straight face.

For a moment, Cass was floored; Lesley had never been risqué before. Then she threw her head back and laughed out loud. They moved through the glass doors and into the store. The day was going to be just great, Cass knew.

They managed to get something for everyone on their lists without having to leave the store, and at five thirty, they stumbled outside, burdened with large bags. Making their way to the front of the Garden, they were elated to snag a cab that was just disgorging its passengers. They high-fived as they piled into the back; it certainly beat lugging their packages onto the train. Not even the smell of stale sweat that permeated the taxi could stifle their spirits.

The mood continued at the apartment where Cass put a calypso Christmas album on the stereo. Although the rhythms were new to Lesley, the words were the same. Filling the rooms with an affecting combination of spirituality and temporality, they harmonized with the Mighty Sparrow:

Oh, there's no place like home for the holidays,
For no matter how far away you roam ...

After they had eaten supper and wrapped their purchases, they showered and put on their pajamas. That way, Lesley reasoned, if they were tired after decorating the tree, they could go straight to bed.

They lugged several boxes of ornaments and lights from the top of the coat closet. A six-foot pine, positioned to reflect in the mirror, flooded the living room with fragrance. While they decorated, they sipped wine and Cass described for Lesley the Christmases she had spent as a child in Antigua.

"At home," she explained, "Christmas is more than a day; it's a whole season that lasts until New Year's." She complimented the British who'd had the good sense to declare the day after Christmas a holiday, designated Boxing Day. "Who could get up for work after all that food and cake, not to mention the liquor, anyway?" she asked.

She told Lesley that when she was a little girl, there was no Santa Claus bringing gifts from the North Pole. Everybody knew it was Father Christmas who brought presents from England, the mother country.

Lesley salivated as Cass described the smells that emanated from her grandmother's kitchen: the clove-studded hams, the garlic-seasoned pork, the head-lightening, rum-soaked cakes and puddings that were washed down with home-made sorrel or ginger beer.

Refilling their glasses, they toasted old-fashioned Christmases.

Every few years, the house would be painted in time for the season, Cass continued. Lesley could picture the house as Cass described it: the new lace curtains billowing at the well-washed windows, squeaky new linoleum on the kitchen floor and a freshly starched and ironed linen cloth on the table. All the good things would be taken out of the cabinet: china and cutlery, glasses that matched and bore no nicks and chips, fine serving dishes. Even the ceramic fruit that sat on the dining table would be washed and buffed to its former shine.

And best of all, Cass said, the red poinsettias flowered in the warm sunshine.

By this time, the tree was done and they sat back to admire their handiwork. Cass had inherited all her mother's ornaments when Mrs. Shortman returned home, and she recalled and shared with Lesley the history of each set. Atop the tree was a cherubic black Santa, holding a list and checking it twice, and shiny red candy canes were interspersed with delicate crystal snowflakes and spiky gold balls. Six miniature stockings also adorned the tree, representing each family member. And through the tinsel, white lights blinked peace on earth and goodwill to men.

Lesley suggested they turn off the lamps and enjoy the illumination from the tree after they finished the bottle. She draped herself on the sofa in her favorite position, supine on the cushions, with her long legs draped over the arm. Cass sat on the floor, her head resting against the side of the couch. For a long while there was a companionable silence, as they listened to the stereo and watched the lights create happy patterns on the walls and furniture.

Abstractedly, Cass began caressing the foot that lay close to her shoulder. Then, turning slightly, she began to kiss Lesley's left foot, running her lips up and down the arched instep. There was no objection, no rejection, and, suddenly bold, Cass lightly bit into the soft, fleshy heel. She heard Lesley moan. Swiveling around, Cass turned her attention to the other foot, now biting, now nuzzling. Lesley sighed loudly and shuddered, her body shifting on the cushions.

Cass stood and pulled her down onto the rug. She sank to her knees and began kissing her way up Lesley's legs, raising them to nip at the little hollows at the backs of her knees. Lesley was whimpering constantly now and her body jerked spasmodically. As she gently pushed up Lesley's gown, Cass discovered that she wore no underwear. Cass desperately wanted to inhale her, to make acquaintance with the contours of her hips, to sample the flavor of her flesh. Filled with an unnamed urgency, she forced herself to stop, however.

"Are you drunk?" she inquired, forcing Lesley to open her eyes.

"No," she husked. "Why?"

"Because I want you to remember this in the morning," Cass replied.

14

For as long as I live, I will remember last night, Lesley told herself the following day. How could she forget the lovemaking that was not only physically shattering, but emotionally satisfying, as well? She had not made love in more than two years, not since Gene had become sick, and she had grown accustomed to seeing herself in a non-sexual light. Cass had reminded her that she was a woman in her prime.

How many times had she said to herself in the past, "If only the foreplay lasted longer"? Well, it finally had. For as long as Lesley could stand it, Cass had teased and toyed with her most private places until she heard herself keening from the intensity of her pleasure. Cass had whispered to her, "Go ahead, pet; go ahead," following Lesley's naked body across the rug as she jerked and flailed.

Then when Cass put her mouth on her, slowly threading her flesh through the gap in her teeth ¾oh¾ Lesley had thought she would die. Two years of pent-up feelings had condensed into that one little piece of her. She was a tiny, erect switch just waiting to be flicked. And the warm wetness that was Cass's tongue was all the flick she needed. It felt so different from a calloused fingertip or lips fringed by bristly male hair. It was so soft, so hard, so good!!

Afterwards, as she lay panting, little tremors still coursing through her body, Cass had drawn herself up to lie on top of her. Cass kissed her neck, her eyes and her ears, then cupped her face and pressed her lips hard upon hers. Lesley could smell and taste herself, and the sensation was deeply erotic. Gene had usually started lovemaking by kissing her and working his way south. She'd always enjoyed it, but this reverse approach delighted her even more.

When Lesley was absolutely still, Cass had gone to the bathroom, returning with a damp washcloth, and had wiped her face and neck, then her thighs. Then they moved to the bedroom and, for the first time, shared the big bed. Silently, they had snuggled under the comforter, drowsy and satiated.

47

Toward morning, Cass had awakened Lesley by running urgent hands over the curves of her body. Taking Lesley's sloping breasts into her hands, Cass gently sucked each, lightly tugging at the turgid nipples. Sensation shot through Lesley like lasers reaching into her body, and she mewled her delight.

Turning her over onto her stomach, Cass brushed aside Lesley's hair and began to lick the back of her neck, slowly moving down her spine toward her peach-shaped bottom. She left a trail of goose bumps as the damp spots cooled in the open air, but this only enhanced Lesley's awareness of her body. Then Cass gently spread Lesley's thighs, parting her with her fingers and sucking up her soft center. Arching her back ferally, Lesley tossed her head from side to side as she clawed the sheets.

She might've been drunk, but it was with pleasure. There would be no hangover, however.

While Lesley slept, Cass had kept vigil. Leaning on one elbow, she watched her lover's face come into focus as dawn faintly lightened the room. In repose, Lesley looked young, defenseless, and Cass's heart constricted with the knowledge that she wanted to wake up with her for the rest of their lives.

She had loved the innocence in Lesley, and now she loved the passion. Cass had known it was there: in her latently sexual gait, the sensuous drape of her long legs over the sofa, and the low, confidential quality of her voice. But Cass had been prepared to draw it out slowly, and she had anticipated doing so. Discovering that Lesley was such a receptive lover, so passionate, so expressive, was like receiving a loosely wrapped gift.

Cass finally finished her contemplation and, getting up quietly, took a shower. She laved her body lovingly, memories of the night making her movements slow and languid. She struggled to resist going back into the bedroom and making love to Lesley again. Instead she dressed and left the apartment, in search of breakfast.

When she returned with fresh offerings from H&H Bagels and steaming cups of coffee from her favorite deli, Cass heard the clock radio playing. The bed had been made, and she could hear the shower going. Knocking briefly at the bathroom door, she entered and asked: "Need help with anything?"

Sliding the shower door open a fraction, Lesley shouted: "Get out of here."

"Why?"

"Because."

Cass sat on the bed until Lesley emerged, properly attired in her terry robe. Again, Cass had to fight to remain seated, to stifle the urge to throw her arms around her. But she could not control the big smile that lit her face.

Lesley raised an eyebrow. "What're you so happy about?"

"You," Cass answered. She patted the area beside her and Lesley sat down. "I'm very happy this morning. Aren't you?"

"Yes, I am." She smiled shyly.

"You know, Lesley, I didn't think you'd be like this. So receptive." She paused, as Lesley's skin tightened and glowed in a blush.

"Honest, I was prepared to wait ¾ a whole year if I had to ¾ until you felt comfortable enough. I really expected some sort of objection. Some ... some heterosexual revulsion. 'Gosh-I-don't-know-if-I-can-do-*that*.' You know what I mean?"

"Well, to tell the truth, I am a little surprised at myself," Lesley laughed self-consciously. "But I've been thinking about it a lot since we had that discussion. *A lot.* I thought it was something I'd have to *talk* myself into. And if I couldn't¾well, I would have done it anyway. Just for you. Don't look so surprised," she laughed, as Cass's eyebrows shot up.

"But there we were, sharing Christmas memories, decorating the tree, and drinking wine¾doing 'couple' things¾and it just felt so ... natural."

She bit her lip. "I believe every straight woman thinks about it at some point in her life¾even in passing. Making love with another woman, I mean. But I couldn't see myself *agreeing* to do it. I always imagined there'd be some sort of role-playing going on¾that the 'masculine' partner would dominate the 'feminine' one. Am I making sense?"

"Yeah," Cass nodded her head, "you mean where the 'dyke' *forced* you."

"I guess. But it wasn't like that. I was comfortable enough not just to agree, but to *enjoy* making love with you."

Cass was full, overwhelmed by what the admission must have cost

Lesley.

"I love you," she said, finally, pulling her close. "You know that?"

"I love you, too, Cass."

They laughed shakily. Then, all briskness, they went out to the kitchen to have breakfast before the coffee became completely cold.

"When are we going to open our gifts?" Lesley inquired. They had agreed to exchange personal gifts at the apartment and take a "safe" gift to Lesley's house.

Cass insisted on taking pictures of the tree before they unwrapped the presents. She went first, starting with a package she knew was a book. When she opened it and discovered a copy of *Erotique Noire,* her light eyes lit up with pleasure. An exquisite brocade bookmark lay between the pages.

"I've been meaning to get this," Cass smiled. "Now, when you're not here, I have something to compensate."

"But you haven't looked at the page," Lesley protested.

Cass looked down, then looked up. The poem Lesley had marked was titled 'Teach Me.' She leaned over and kissed Lesley on the lips. "It'll be my pleasure," she said seriously. "But there's a great deal you'll have to teach me, too. Agreed?"

"Agreed."

The second gift was not so easy to figure out, and they had a few moments of fun as Cass speculated on what it might be.

"Just open it." Lesley was like a kid struggling to contain herself. "You're going to like it."

Cass just stared.

"Wow!" she said finally.

It was a carving of two female figures. A single, full-breasted torso supported two heads, one resting against the other's cheek in an attitude of repose. The sheen of the polished black wood made the piece seem almost animated. It was bizarrely beautiful.

"I commissioned it," Lesley said, delighted at Cass's stunned response. "I got the idea from a painting I'd once seen called 'Symbiosis,' and I had a man I know, a Native American, make it for me. I think he did a great job, considering he had only about two weeks to do it."

"He certainly did, and you did a fine job choosing it. I know this is going to become my favorite piece. I think I'll call it 'Us.'"

Lesley didn't bother with the ritual guessing; she simply tore the paper off her first gift, the flat, oblong one that Cass suggested she open first. A large padded envelope held a page, beautifully matted and framed, of a little dark girl, braids peeping from under a bright purple beret that matched her windbreaker. Her face wreathed in smiles, she was running toward some unseen person at full tilt through a pile of red, gold and brown fall leaves.

"This is me?" Lesley asked, laughing.

"It's the way I imagine you were," Cass answered. "I saw it in a children's book and cut the page out. You couldn't tell, all dressed up as it is."

"Well, fall is certainly my time, but I don't know if I was ever that happy as a kid," Lesley smiled ruefully. "I'm doing better as an adult, though."

This was certainly not the mood Cass had intended to evoke, so she clapped her hands briskly   and shouted, "Next."

The little box was undisguised, and Lesley knew it contained a piece of jewelry. She smiled at Cass as she hefted it playfully. On the red velvet lay an antique-looking gold ring. "Oooh," she whispered, picking it up to admire the pattern. Then she saw the words: *Vous et Nul Autre.* "You and no other." Her eyes filled as she lifted them to Cass.

"What'd I do wrong *now*?" Cass asked, dramatically slumping over and making Lesley laugh through the threatened tears. She helped Lesley undo the long chain she wore around her neck and slip the ring on. They understood that it was too early in their relationship to be fielding questions, and Cass preferred that Lesley keep it close to her heart, anyway.

They hugged in a flurry of thank-yous and Merry Christmases, while, on the radio, Joe Tex was promising to make every day feel like Christmas for his woman.

15

C ass had to mail some packages and they were late making the train. Quiet during the trip, each was busy with her own thoughts.

Cass was nervous at meeting Lesley's children and slightly annoyed about it. "Well," she tried to excuse herself, "I've never had to cultivate anyone's kids before."

In the past, she generally had steered clear of women with baggage, as she called it: kids, boyfriends, dependent parents, addictions of any kind, a history of unemployment.

"All that running and this is where I end up: three kids, a dead husband and a *straight* woman. Nice going, Fish," she congratulated herself.

But when she caught a glance of that straight woman, tinted by the already waning light outside the train window, Cass's heart leaped, and she knew she'd brave ten children and the ghosts of six husbands to keep her.

Lesley had no immediate intention of telling her children about the relationship she shared with Cass. She couldn't explain it, anyway, and there was no sense in confusing them about their mother so soon after their father's death. While she was confident that she and Cass would behave with propriety, she worried, however, that her kids would see through their platonic front. She was suddenly conscious of the way Cass looked at her and, after last night, she worried that she, too, might have become transparent.

When they drove up to Lesley's house, a neatly maintained colonial, there was a weathered Buick Riviera sitting in the driveway. "Seth's home," Lesley said quietly. Turning off the ignition and opening the car door, she exclaimed with pleasure, "And Dow's here, too." They both heard the piano chords.

Cass had never seen photographs of Lesley's children. As affectionate and devoted as she was, Lesley was not the type to assault a person with pictures of her family. Entering the living room, where Dow sat at the piano and Seth lay draped, exactly like his mother, over the sofa, Cass was forced to blink rapidly.

The old saying about boys resembling their mothers certainly held up here, she thought. Although they were both lighter in complexion than their mother, the young men had Lesley's tall, strong build. Seth seemed a bit shorter than Dow, but that might have been because he was more muscular. Their faces were masculine versions of their mother, and Cass wanted to laugh in recognition. Had she met them on New Year's Eve in Times Square, she would have known they were Lesley's sons. They were striking young men.

They hugged their mother and shook hands with Cass.

"Nice to meet you, Miss Shortman," Seth smiled shyly. "I've heard a lot about you."

"And I you," Cass said, smiling in turn. Turning to Dow, she continued, "And you must be the tycoon." They all laughed and she felt her nervousness dissipate. They're just boys, she told herself; beautiful boys.

While Lesley and the boys went outside to get the presents from the car, Cass admired her surroundings. Lesley really had been busy this past week. The cherry wood furniture gleamed; it was old, heavy, but beautifully finished. The brocade cushions were worn but comfortable, their colors picked up in the burgundy rug that covered most of the floor and the patterned drapes at the windows. Everything about the room said comfort, in both the familial and financial sense, and Cass wondered how Lesley could bear to spend so much time in her suddenly-small Manhattan apartment.

She crossed the room and studied the photos displayed atop the piano. The largest frame showed Lesley leaning on a golf-cart, next to a man who was obviously Gene. Cass's first response was shocked surprise. She had expected a tall, handsome man, someone who complemented Lesley; but Gene was a man of medium height, stocky, with a face the color and texture of a bleached brown paperbag. Cass smiled instinctively. He had that sort of face: warm, reassuring, honest. He was the kind of man with whom she would have liked to be friends, and she suddenly missed her brother Luke.

Next to this frame was a green enamel oval from which Generes postured. It had to be her; she looked just like her father, down to the freckles sprinkled across her nose and cheekbones. She was not beautiful like her brothers, but she worked hard with what she had been given. Her long brown hair was piled atop her head and her makeup, skillfully applied, made her almost pretty. She was tall, however, like her mother.

Matching frames displayed the boys. Dow's photo, a head shot, did justice to his expressive face, the smooth brown forehead lightly dewed with perspiration. Cass judged the picture to be about three years old based on his haircut. Seth was pictured, arms folded, on a racing bike. Even under his helmet, his good looks were obvious and his body was beautifully sculpted.

The photos seemed carefully selected to showcase the Gorton children's personalities and interests, Cass thought. Seth, the brawny athlete; Dow, the artist; and Generes, the poser, style compensating for substance.

There were additional photos on the mantel and she moved to examine them. "Ugh! American Gothic," was Cass's reaction to a homely pair who had to be the Gorton grandparents. Another couple were obviously the Hillarys. Cass had expected Lesley's mother to be frumpily dressed, a woman who looked Puritanical and cold. She was surprised to find that Lesley's mother was a tall, brown-skinned woman, whose elegant tailored suit enhanced rather than hid her shapely figure. Her smile, partially shaded by her hat, seemed deeply suggestive. Although Lesley was darker, she resembled her mother, and Cass was reassured to know that her woman would still be a looker at 60. Mr. Hillary, tall, thin and serious, stood half-hidden behind his wife. The last was a group shot of Lesley's sister, Lana, who also resembled their mother, with her husband, in military dress, and their two teenage daughters.

But they all receded into inconsequence before a large black-and-white of Lesley. She wore a long flowered skirt, modest halter, hoop earrings and a perfectly shaped Afro. A snake bracelet was coiled around her slim left arm and her hands were linked peacefully in her lap. Her legs crossed, painted toenails peeped from cork-soled clogs. She epitomized early seventies chic. But it was her eyes, serene and clear as she gazed into the camera, that held Cass and made her yearn, unreasonably, for the years she had missed with Lesley.

It was hard to believe that at the time this picture was taken, Lesley was already a wife and mother, while she, Cass, was probably running around campus, trying out her sexuality and looking for causes. She suddenly felt gauche, unformed, despairing even; how could she compete with Lesley's past, which suddenly seemed full, significant, positively loaded with Kodak moments.

Luckily, Lesley hurried back in just then, calling gaily to Cass to come see upstairs. There used to be three bedrooms on the second floor, Lesley explained, as they mounted the stairs, but they had converted one into a den after the boys were relocated to the attic.

Painted in black and white, the attic was artfully remodeled to take advantage of the sloping roof and deep corners. Mudcloth curtains and window cushions gave it an ethnic yet manly feel. Jackets and gym bags were tossed on the twin beds and the scent of Farenheit lingered in the air. Backgammon tiles littered one night table. The room looked like the boys had never left home.

Cass moved to inspect a large sepia print of Bob Marley over one bed. "Dow's, I assume?" She looked questioningly at Lesley, who shook her head.

"He's not the only musical one in the family, you know. Seth plays the recorder."

"Really?" Cass replied. "And what does Generes play?"

"The fool mostly," was Lesley's wry reply. Cass had the feeling she wasn't joking, which startled her, for Lesley was not the type to criticize her kids openly.

Generes wasn't expected until tomorrow and was spending only one night, so Cass was taking her room for the weekend. Papered in cool blue with a muted silver border, the room was sleekly modern. The drapes, comforter and rug were a metallic shade of grey, and a mobile of silver wires and pieces of quartz hung from one corner of the ceiling. A series of black and white photos lined the far wall.

"Generes did these?" Cass inquired.

"In her Gordon Parks era," Lesley nodded.

"They're good!" Cass exclaimed, thinking that she would have to reassess Generes.

"She's good at everything, but stays with nothing," Lesley sighed. "She decorated the attic, too. ... I'll ask Seth to bring your things up. Let me show you the rest."

The little den was cozy: overstuffed corduroy armchairs, a desk with a computer system, and an L-shaped bookcase that also housed a compact sound system. A hand-made rag rug covered the polished floor. "Oh my, this is so charming," Cass exclaimed. "I love it."

At the end of the hall was Lesley's bedroom. For some reason, Cass dreaded going in there. It seemed so personal, so *married*, somehow. She followed Lesley hesitantly.

Facing the door was the bed, the black walnut headboard simply carved, but with a glorious swatch of tapestry cushioning the middle. An armoire stood to the left and a night table to the right, while a TV cart sat at the end of the bed. The linens, in graduated hues of green, matched the vertical blinds. A recliner and hassock faced the far wall. Coming properly into the room, Cass could see the mirrored double dresser on which sat a lovely Lladro piece, but her eyes were drawn to the light coming in from the West wall. A stained-glass window, hectagonal in shape, its panes of emerald, red and gold, was burnished by the now-fading sun. The colored rays played over the far end of the carpet, lending the long room a cathedral-like quality.

Her silence spoke as Cass turned round and round to admire; it was truly a lovely room. Yet Cass knew they would never make love here, for if, somehow, she could get past the presence-of-God atmosphere, she'd never get over the picture of Gene who stared benevolently at her from the wall above the bed.

Despite this conviction, however, late that night she lay awake in her borrowed bed and wished she could be there to see the morning sun dapple Lesley's body through the stained-glass window.

16

Christmas was going well, Lesley thought. Her family was happy; her lover was laughing; everyone seemed to be getting along. It was so different from the last two years.   She sighed, but not unhappily. His last Christmas, Gene had had to be helped to the table, where he attempted to make conversation, but unable to eat anything. That he was there at all was a testament to his determination; he *wanted* to spend his last Christmas with his family.

When all the festivities were over, he retired to the daybed on the enclosed porch and left it only to return to the hospital. He was buried the day before New Year's Eve.

This year, Seth had invited Yoline, his girlfriend, and Dow, too, had a guest, the girl at whose house he had spent Thanksgiving. (He refused to call her his girlfriend, however.) They were all in high spirits.

Lesley wondered if the kids' gaiety was born of relief, a sigh that the suffering ¾for everyone¾ finally was over. Whatever it was, she was simply grateful that this felt like a real Christmas. She missed Gene, no doubt about that, but they had mourned enough and he would be the first to tell them to get on with their lives. Before coming downstairs that morning, she had vowed to be thankful for what she had, instead of brooding about what she had lost.

After Seth and Dow returned from taking gifts to their grandparents, Generes arrived amidst much hoopla. Though Lesley tried gently to calm her, everything delighted Generes¾loudly.

Introduced as an old friend of her mother's, Cass had been greeted like a long-lost aunt, as Generes hugged her tightly. Over her head, Lesley rolled her eyes at Cass, mutely asking for forbearance.

They opened presents, oohing and aahing and feigning envy, and Generes hugged Cass yet again, thanking her profusely for the bottle of *L'Air du Temps* she had gotten. Lesley had told Cass that it was not necessary; she didn't know the kids, after all. But Cass had insisted on getting stocking stuffers for all of them.

They abandoned plans for a sit-down dinner and helped themselves all afternoon to whatever took their fancy, in no particular order. Lesley and Cass had begun cooking the night before and had gotten up early to finish. Their efforts were stupendous: chicken breasts stuffed with spinach, sun dried tomatoes, mushrooms and garlic, and a succulent roast beef; wild rice, savory stuffing, and a potato-zucchini casserole smothered in cheese; asparagus spears and glazed carrots; a cheesecake and a pound cake infused with brandy; water crackers and Brie. It was a gustatory free for all.

By early evening, they were all slightly tipsy, plenty stuffed and totally enervated. Even Generes was quiet, probably overcome by the liquor-soaked dessert. Collapsing onto the floor and the comfortable chairs of the living room, they persuaded Dow to play.

They pressed Seth to accompany him on the recorder, but he refused modestly. So Dow played alone, moving easily through his considerable repertoire and encircling the room with gentle chords that lulled his audience into that common, yet highly individual, feeling of nostalgia that is indescribably Christmas.

When he segued from Nat King Cole's "Blue Gardenia" into one of Cass's favorite songs, she sighed with pleasure. Across the darkened room and above the bodies slumped on the floor, she gazed toward Lesley as she sang along with Dow:

> *I offer you a love that has no strings,*
> *No spoken vows to clip your wings.*
> *A love that touches you, but never clings.*
> *For pleasing you is all I have in mind.*
> *Here, with me, I know you'll find*
> *A love that's strong, but not the choking kind.*
> *Stay awhile, and live with me.*
> *Just stick around and we'll see*
> *What happens.*
> *For what will be, will be.*
> *And we'll live each day as it comes.*

17

Lesley finally revived enough to serve eggnog and coffee, then suggested that Seth and Dow take their guests home before it got much later. When Seth backed the old Riviera out of the garage, Generes discovered her mother's new car and insisted on taking it around the block. Lesley tried to dissuade her, citing the hour and suggesting that she wait until the next day. But Generes had already flown to the kitchen where the keys hung on a rack. Not wanting to spoil the evening or make a scene in front of Cass, Lesley finally capitulated and pleaded with her to be careful. It was bitterly cold and the roads were sure to be slick with ice.

Cass began to understand Lesley's cryptic comment of the previous night, but she sought to calm her: "She'll be all right, I'm sure. It's not like she doesn't know the roads." She was thrown, however, when Lesley replied, "Sure, she also knew the roads when she crashed Dow's car two years ago."

Silently, they cleared the table, wrapping leftovers in foil trays that could be popped into the oven for reheating next day and loading the dishwasher. Brewing fresh coffee, they carried mugs to the unlighted living room to wait for the kids' return.

"I have to admit, I can't understand how you can leave this beautiful house so often, Lesley," Cass shook her head.

"It *is* nice, isn't it?" Lesley sighed. "Gene was a real handyman, you know. Always remodeling, putting in this, taking out that. Even the furniture we have now, for instance. He got most of it in antique stores and refurbished it. My father taught him, actually. Dad was a furniture maker, a good one, and he made a lot of money back when people liked things built to last. He works mostly for churches now. We got the stained-glass window from his workshop."

She continued a bit sadly. "But you know, Cass, as much as I love this place and used to take pride in making it nice ¾ it's just a house now. After Gene died and Seth went back to Queens ¾ he'd moved back home for a bit ¾ it was just me, and I often thought I'd go crazy in the silence. Even now, I don't know why I keep it." She paused. "For occasions like this, I guess. If Dow were a little older, I'd give it to him, I think."

"Well, maybe Generes will get married soon, and she might like to live here," Cass offered.

"Speaking of which," Lesley said, squinting to see the mantel clock, "this little spin is getting longer by the minute. It's not that I don't trust her, as such," she told Cass apologetically, "but Generes often doesn't think, and the older she gets the bigger the risks are somehow. The only place I feel she's really safe, believe it or not, is when she's at work."

"But she's a flight attendant!" Cass exclaimed.

"Yes, but *someone else* is flying the plane."

They dissolved into laughter and the anxiety was momentarily dissipated.

"I've noticed that she calls you Lesley, while the boys call you Mom," Cass commented. "How come?"

"I don't even notice that anymore," Lesley said. "We didn't live together as a family¾a nuclear family¾until Generes was about five or so. She and Dow were born when Gene was in the service, and the three of us lived with my parents. So she grew up thinking that Momma and Dad were her parents, and I was her big sister or something. She just started calling me Lesley, like my parents did.

"Gene tried to get her to stop when he came home, but she'd call me Mommy only when he was there to hear her. I let it slide," she said offhandedly. "I grew up in a strict household, and I didn't want to hassle my daughter over such a small thing."

By now, Cass had learned that remaining silent was the best way to get Lesley to talk.

"She and Gene used to fight all the time," Lesley continued. "She really, really, resented him coming into our lives and taking her away from her grandfather. Dad might not have known how to be a father, but he was crazy about the kids ¾ at least the first two. For some reason, they never took to Seth as much ¾ and he's such a great kid." She frowned, perplexed.

"Anyway, my mother taught the kids to play. Seventy years old, and she's still the music director of her church, you know," Lesley said admiringly. "I still don't play well and I took piano for years. And

Lana's hardly any better. Sometimes I think the reason Momma wasn't crazy about us was that neither of us was really talented."

She laughed self-consciously. "How did I get onto this subject, anyway?"

"Doesn't matter," Cass replied, going over to perch on the arm of Lesley's chair. "*I'm* crazy about you." Holding Lesley's chin, she tipped her face and kissed her forehead. Lesley recognized Cass's maternal gesture for what it was, comfort, reassurance, love —without the heat that often flamed through her eyes. She knew the heat was there, but she was grateful that it was leashed — for now.

They sat like that until they heard tires crunching the frost that bordered the driveway. Cass moved away from Lesley, who sighed unconsciously with relief. But it was the boys returning, and when she heard their voices at the kitchen door, Lesley was positively aghast.

"You let her take the car?" Dow was incredulous, while Seth simply shook his head disbelievingly. "Don't you learn anything, Ma? You know Generes. When did she leave here, anyway?"

"Right after you did. She took the keys and said she was only going around the block. She just wanted to try it out ...." She was babbling, frightened, imagining the worst and remembering Gene all over again.

Tears were springing to Lesley's eyes, and Cass felt sorry for her but said nothing. It occurred to her that Lesley was a bit intimidated by Dow, who, she had observed, could be moody. Seth wasn't saying anything either, but then Generes hadn't wrecked *his* car, Cass thought wryly. For some reason, she was certain the accident had been Generes' fault.

"We drove to Fresh Meadows *and* Astoria *and* back, and she's not here yet," Dow continued sarcastically. "Don't worry, nothing's happened to her. *Around* her, maybe, but not *to* her."

Pleasantly enough, however, he bent and kissed Cass on the cheek, "Goodnight, Miss Shortman. Merry Christmas." Then, calmly, he kissed his mother goodnight, turned on his heel and went upstairs.

When his brother left the room, Seth spoke up. "She's all right, Mom," he reassured. "She probably just stopped at one of her friends or something. She'll be here soon." Then casting his eyes around the kitchen, he inquired, "Is there anything here to eat?"

Pulling chairs, the three sat at the kitchen table to wait. Lesley was silent, staring out into the darkness beyond the window, but Cass kept up a conversation with Seth as he ate chicken and casserole, followed by a slab of cake.

He would graduate the following spring, Seth told her with satisfaction, and he was going to France on a bike tour in the summer. That's why his mother had bought him Speedo gear for Christmas, he explained. He told her about his plans to teach junior high while he pursued his master's in secondary mathematics education. He had been mentoring in a high school since he was a sophomore, he explained, and had realized that many of the problems he encountered at that level could have been successfully headed off a few years earlier. Further, Seth said, when he realized that a disproportionate number of junior-high teachers were female, he knew he had found a place where he could make a difference.

Cass was impressed. With her penchant for understatement, Lesley had merely described Seth as a nice boy; she had never said he was this smart or socially conscious. Cass determined then to break her professional code and personally make sure that Seth was effectively placed. This young hopeful was one fledgling she didn't want to become another first-year casualty of the public schools.

But all she actually said was, "I'll see what's out there, but you know you won't get rich teaching, don't you?"

"That's okay," he said seriously, "my brother's gonna be rich. He'll watch my back."

Hearing a car crunch into the driveway, they all automatically looked at the kitchen clock. It was 1:07 A.M. Generes had been gone for nearly three hours. She came through the kitchen door, her color high, exhilarated.

"Lesley, that is *some* ride!" she exclaimed, shrugging out of her coat.

There was no response and, sensing the mood, her eyes widened in fear as she whispered, "What's the matter? Did something happen?"

Lesley looked at her dully. "You said you were going around the block, Generes."

"Oh!" she laughed shortly, visibly relieved. "Well I was, but you know how that car goes. Whoosh! Before I knew it, I was in Elmont. ..."

"Figures," Seth said under his breath.

"Yeah, I went to see Grandad and Gramma. He was thrilled to see me," she went on. "He really likes the car, too, Lesley. Said it was a good buy."

"You went to Dad's and you didn't even call, huh? Do you even *know* how long you've been gone? People were *worried* about you," Lesley said, getting angry.

"Look, time went by, all right. I didn't realize how late it was getting. I'm fine! Is anybody ever going to forget I had an accident? I've told you already¾it wasn't my fault."

She stomped toward the door, then paused dramatically and inquired, "It's still okay with you if I sleep in your room, isn't it?"

"Kids," Lesley said conspiratorially to Cass in an effort to cover her embarrassment. Cass shook her head as though she understood the burdens of motherhood and the caprices of children.

"Oh, well, she's leaving tomorrow, so let's just go to bed," Lesley continued. "Do you need anything before we go up?"

Mounting the stairs, each was privately relieved that Generes lived hundreds of miles away.

18

Neither Cass nor Dow came down on Sunday morning to say goodbye to Generes. Cass pretended to be asleep, while Dow simply appeared downstairs, without excuses, *after* Generes had been picked up by her friend.

Cass had found herself angry the night before. Angry that Lesley's plans for a good Christmas¾which she certainly deserved¾had been ruined by her daughter's lack of consideration. She had wanted Lesley's kids to like her, and she had wanted to like them, as well. But no matter how she told herself she was overreacting to a small incident, she could not erase the memory of Lesley, her eyes filling her face, silently hoping that her daughter's absence did not mean another loss.

When Cass finally went down, Lesley was again smiling easily with the boys, who sat around the table eating, while she packed food into microwave containers. The kids were leaving in the early afternoon since they both had to work next day. Dow teased Cass for oversleeping, chiding her for not being able to handle her liquor, and Seth offered to make her breakfast. An air of normalcy reigned and, unconsciously, Cass sighed with relief. By the time they loaded their gifts, packed into large brown Macy's bags, into Seth's car, along with their overnight bags and care packages, Cass was genuinely sorry to see them go.

"How come Dow never went into the music business?" she inquired, as Lesley turned from watching the car go up the street, its exhaust like a white scarf waving in the bitter cold.

"My son is practical," Lesley answered, "to a fault! He says every other black kid can sing, dance, or play an instrument, and talent's not enough to live on. The boy likes gravy on his grits, you see."

They laughed ruefully and went back to the warmth of the kitchen.

"So what are we going to do with the rest of the day?" Cass inquired, as they unloaded the dishwasher.

"Don't know. What do you want to do? Take a drive out to Jones Beach?" Lesley asked desultorily. "But it'll be dark soon ... and it's so cold," she answered herself.

"I'm a city girl," Cass reminded her. "I have no idea what to do out here."

"To tell the truth, Cass, even I don't know what to do with myself out here anymore. I can't work in my garden, obviously. And if there's nothing that needs cleaning, I'm at a loss. Most of the time, I come back here just for the sake of decency."

"Decency?"

"Well, I figured that you must need some space in your apartment ... some time to be alone."

"I've been alone for years," Cass said seriously. "It's not all it's cracked up to be." For a long moment, she gazed at Lesley. "I was rather hoping that I'd never have to be alone again."

"In that case," Lesley said quietly, "let's go home."

The evening train was deserted going into Manhattan. In comfortable silence, Lesley lounged against Cass, who stared out the window enjoying the passing lights of a suburban Christmas.

"Cass?"

"Hmm?"

"When did you know you were gay?"

"You mean when *didn't* I know I was gay?"

"Seriously?" Lesley struggled to sit up. "You always knew?"

"Well, I discovered it at the same time you realized you were hetero, I suppose. I was¾ what¾about 11 years old, and my parents had gone to a funeral," Cass recalled. "This girl, Jacintha, was supposed to be minding me, but I couldn't find her. I wandered into my brothers' room, for some reason, and there she was with Matthew. She was bent over, her dress thrown up over her back, and he was holding her breasts in his hands. I stood there watching and they didn't even notice me ¾ they were going at it so hard. At that moment," Cass said gravely, "I wanted with all my heart to be Matthew."

"And when did you have your first sexual experience?" Lesley inquired, looking at her with frank curiosity now.

"What's this? Twenty questions?" Cass laughed, a bit guardedly.

"I'm just curious, that's all," Lesley admitted. "I want to know about 'your past.'"

"OK, OK. You're not going to believe this, but I had to wait until *college* to get laid. It started at a dance, a Sadie Hawkins dance, during sophomore year. I had to take tickets at the door, and I stuck around to hear the band because I was friends with one of the singers.

"They were playing 'Help Me Make It Through the Night,' and all of a sudden, this girl came over to me and said, 'May I?' I couldn't believe it! I was embarrassed and tried to move away, and she laughed and asked me what I was afraid of, this was 1970, after all. So I went with her onto the floor. And that was that.

"Her name was Allyson-June Sweeting; everyone called her 'Sweet Thing,'" Cass laughed. "She was a bit of a BAP. She got whatever she wanted, and until senior year, she wanted me." Cass paused. "Last I heard, she was married to a judge and had four kids."

"N-o-o-o!" Lesley interjected disbelievingly.

"Oh, yes!" Cass concluded, highly amused. "And that's all I'm going to say about 'my past' today. I'd rather enjoy my present," she said, gathering up their things as the train pulled into Penn Station, "and look forward to the future."

A number of holiday messages awaited Cass at the apartment and she sat down to play them back and jot down numbers.

The last message was loud and jovial: "Happy Christmas, Cassandra," boomed a thick Barbadian accent. "Girl, is *months* I don't hear from you! You must be getting something, eh? Well, whatever it is you getting, you can bring her Saturday night to the party. 10:00 o'clock. See you."

"Who was *that?*" Lesley asked.

"That was Darlin," Cass laughed. "Actually, his name is Darwin, but because of his accent and his flamboyance, everybody calls him Darlin. He has a New Year's Eve party every year. Want to go?"

Apprehension chased insecurity across Lesley's face. "Who's going to be there?" she asked cautiously.

Cass tried to stifle the rush of annoyance she instinctively felt. "Gays. Straights. *People.* You'll have to get your feet wet some time, you know, pet."

Lesley bit her lip and looked away, and Cass forced herself to affect a conciliatory tone.

"His sister is a marvelous cook," she coaxed. "The food alone is worth going for. And the music is always good¾lots of calypso, lots of oldies. Darlin and Evan, his lover, have been throwing this party for years. Evan died of cancer about seven years ago, but Darlin keeps us the tradition," Cass explained. "Marcus and Sylvie are going, too, so it's not like you won't know anyone there. Sylvie and Darlin are cousins, by the way."

"I don't have anything formal with me, but I'll think about it," Lesley called over her shoulder, heading into the bathroom. She stared in the mirror, conflicted. She knew how Cass felt about her and was growing comfortable accepting and even reciprocating those feelings. But it was one thing to be with her in an intimate, private setting; it was quite another to go to an affair where everyone knew Cass, knew she was gay and, therefore, would know, or assume, they were lovers.

Lesley was ashamed of her feelings. She felt like some sort of reverse Judas, professing her love to Cass and betraying her by withholding the public kiss.

Soaping her limbs under the stinging water, shampooing her hair to get rid of the cooking smells, moisturizing her body after she dried off, she could not rid herself of the feeling of shame. Cass was worth more than this, she told herself. She deserved someone who wasn't self-conscious about loving her.

Cass understood the struggle that Lesley was having with herself. Talking about Allyson-June that afternoon had forced her to remember how she had been at the beginning of that relationship. Shy. Self-conscious. Concerned about what people said about her. And she was *gay,* for God's sake! She resolved not to bring up the subject again that night.

After Cass completed her own ablutions, they agreed to watch *It's a Wonderful Life.* "Call me what you like, but I never get tired of this movie," Cass sighed. "Watching it makes the season complete, somehow."

"I know what you mean," Lesley agreed. "No matter how often *The Sound of Music* is on TV, I watch it, too. I'll swear, 'Not this time,' then I'll stop just to listen to the Mother Superior sing 'Climb Every Mountain,' and that's it. I'm hooked."

They settled down in the bedroom to relish the Christmas classic. Cass sat in the battered, comfortable armchair, with Lesley on a cushion between her legs, a bowl of caramel popcorn perched atop her knees.

As Cass toweled and gently combed out Lesley's hair, they competed with each other to quote the timeless lines.

Later, as they lay spoon-fashion under the goosedown comforter, Cass commented sleepily that it was the best Boxing Day she had enjoyed outside of Antigua.

19

After Lesley's quiet announcement that she would attend Darlin's party, Cass had left the apartment, returning hours later with the flirty black silk dress Lesley was now wearing. Waving aside her protests, Cass then pulled out the suede slingbacks she had combed Lexington Avenue to find and insisted that Lesley try everything on.

The dress was short, leaving bare the little indentations at the backs of her knees that Cass so loved. The high heels flattered Lesley's strong legs and made them appear longer and more sensuous. Unable to resist the allure of the fabric, Lesley twirled, making the skirt rise and billow provocatively. Completing the turn, she faced Cass, who had come upright on the side of the bed, her light-colored eyes narrowed and glinting with passion.

"Yes," she said softly, "yes."

Later that day, Lesley asked Cass how much she had spent, insisting that she had to pay for the outfit.

"Let me tell you something," Cass said quietly, moving to stand in front of Lesley. "Since college I've accepted myself, and I'm comfortable with who I am. And *what* I am. I'm not an envious person, but every so often, I'm *consumed* by envy for straight people. You know why? Because they've got the privilege of showing their feelings, anytime, anywhere, without even thinking about it. Not a privilege; a right!"

Palms up, she searched for words and her voice rose. "You don't know...you don't understand...how it is for me sometimes. The little things. Like the other day when we were waiting for a cab? You looked so cold, I was dying¾dying¾to hug you and pull you inside my coat." She laughed, but not in an amused way. "But could I? My God, Lesley, the most I can do is *wave* goodbye when I get off the train in the morning!"

As her anguish increased, her accent had become distinctly Caribbean.

"You think I'm happy always hiding my feelings?" she asked.

"Pretending that we're 'just good friends'? For whom? For the public? Why should I give a damn about the public? I love you and I want to be able to say it. *And show it!* That's why it's important that you go to this party with me. Because no one there will be judging us.

"So don't ask me what anything costs. OK," she finished. "It's a gift, because I love you and because I'm happy you're going to the party with me. There's no owing between us."

"Thank you," Lesley said.

So here she was now, sweating in the back seat of a cold cab, while Cass chattered excitedly about who they would see at the party and how much fun they would have.

Lesley did not know what she had expected exactly, but it wasn't this. Walking into Darlin's foyer, she had braced herself for shock, perhaps; a bit of discomfort, certainly; maybe even for some embarrassment. But these people were more normal than most of the church people she had grown up with.

Darlin met them, beaming. "Cas-sandra, girl you're alive!" he shouted, hugging her. "And who is this? Lesley? Is so nice to meet you. You been keepin' my friend hide away from me," he laughed.

He wore a burgundy smoking jacket over crushed velvet lounge pants. Although he could not be called good-looking, with his high, domed forehead and graying sideburns, Darlin certainly was distinguished enough to carry off the outfit. Deftly separating her from Cass, he ushered Lesley over to a group of people gathered in the brightly lit and fragrant kitchen. "Everybody, this is Lesley, Cas-sandra's girlfriend," he announced gaily, and the group opened up to welcome her.

Shortly before dinner was served, Cass beckoned Lesley over to meet Marcus and his wife who had just arrived. The family resemblance between Darlin and Sylvie was apparent, and Marcus's wife was expensively dressed and impeccably groomed. Tall and thin, she was a striking woman, and a pretty face would have been gratuitous. As she was, she appeared the perfect foil to Marcus's muscularity and good looks.

"Sylvie," Cass said, drawing Lesley forward, "this is my girlfriend, Lesley." The comma was not lost on anyone.

Smiling warmly and extending her hand, Sylvie said, "Welcome to the family."

Lesley liked her immediately and, relaxing, she smiled in turn, squeezing Sylvie's hand, and then turned to greet Marcus. While Cass and her brother worked the room, drifting from group to group, Sylvie and Lesley sat together talking as though they'd been friends for years. Darlin, noticing them, couldn't help saying slyly to Cass: "Watch yourself. I notice Sylvie horning you, man."

At ten before midnight, a thrill of excitement coursed through the party as Darlin turned on the big-screen television in the living room. Dick Clark's familiar voice was priming the City as it awaited 1994.

"Everybody got a glass?" Darlin was shouting above the excited chatter, moving around professionally with a bottle of champagne in each hand. People began pairing off, and Cass and Marcus made their way back across the room.

"Ten, nine, eight, seven," the crowd chanted, "six, five, four." Lesley felt Cass's arm around her shoulder. "Three, two, one. Happy New Year!" Cass turned her around, pressing her lips to hers. "Happy New Year, pet," she murmured, her throat full. "Happy New Year, Cass," Lesley whispered back, unexpectedly affected.

Someone raised his voice and sang, "Should auld acquaintance be forgot and never brought to mind?" Everyone joined in, loudly, hugging and kissing each other.

Immediately after the New Year was sung in, their host turned up his impressive sound system, and the guests cheered as they surged onto the floor. In a minute, Lesley had picked up the refrain and was singing with the rest of the crowd: "If you can't get a woman, take a man. It's the only solution: take a man."

They were damp and sweaty as they peeled into the warm apartment lobby at precisely 3:00 o'clock. "Was that a fete or was that a fete?" Cass inquired, as they collapsed against the walls of the elevator.

"The best," Lesley said. "I can't tell the last time I enjoyed myself so much."

She could hardly believe that only two years ago her world had been emptied as she laid Gene to rest. But somehow, she was feeling no guilt, only happiness that she could be happy again.

Her dress clung to her and she headed straight to the shower. After Lesley finished, Cass followed her into the tub, singing snatches of the calypsos she had just enjoyed. Running a washcloth over her body, she called to Lesley to bring her something to put on. It was one of her quirks that she never wore a nightshirt twice.

"Here you go," she heard Lesley say. Sliding the doors open, she stared uncomprehendingly at Lesley's cupped palm.

"You said you wanted something to wear," Lesley said seriously, handing Cass the pair of amber earrings she had taken off the dresser.

A sensuous smile played over Cass's face as she stepped out of the tub. Tossing the washcloth in the direction of the sink, she cupped Lesley's face and kissed her lips hungrily. She could feel the passion igniting the champagne in her blood, as she hurriedly backed Lesley into the bedroom and tugged loose the belt of her robe. Tipping her against the bed, Cass straddled her body and kissed her eyes closed.

Lesley could feel an ever-so-slight tingle upon her lids from the toothpaste that flavored Cass's lips, but it was nothing compared to the fire that was now licking inside her. She tossed her head helplessly as Cass's tongue foraged into the hollow of her throat and played with the pulse beating wildly there, then began her little feline sounds as it descended to her tumid nipples. She agonized during its slow, damp descent, its detour into the depression of her navel, across her hip bones and the length of her scar, before finally, finally, it fluttered home. She sucked in her breath and drew up her knees in welcome.

For long, lazy minutes Cass alternately inhaled and laved her, making Lesley arch for the contact she teasingly withheld. Then, changing her approach suddenly, she pointed and hardened her tongue, using it to spear the oyster that was offered her. As Lesley came, mewling and bucking, Cass stretched out upon her lover and ground her body tightly into hers.

Their skins finally cooled and they eeled themselves, naked, under the heavy comforter, settling into the posture they now naturally assumed.

Just before they dozed off, Lesley murmured against Cass's shoulder: "Cass? Have you ever made love with a man?"

"Uh-uh," Cass shook her head sleepily. "Too kinky."

20

Never particularly upbeat in the morning, Cass became less so as cold day succeeded cold day, and snowstorm after snowstorm punished the Tri-state area. She was sick of the weather and hated coming downstairs to face the piles of grey-black snow that refused to melt. On days like these, she tried to conjure up memories of long, sweaty summer evenings spent near the fountain at Lincoln Center, but even her imagination refused to thaw. The schools were closed yet again, and she missed Lesley, who had gone to Westbury.

Whenever Lesley went home for one of Dow's visits, Cass would use the time to catch up on the phone with Sylvie or to call home. Invariably she would also go to Astoria to have dinner with Darlin.

This time, Lesley had gone home, with Seth, to take care of their almost-frozen pipes and the roof of the sun-porch, which threatened to collapse under the weight of snow it had accumulated. Unable to find a workman to come to the house, she had literally carved a path through the yard so that her son and his friends could get to the back and hack the snow off the roof. No sooner had the boys departed than a new storm dumped another five inches, obscuring her back-breaking labor. Next day, she was out again with her shovel and salt, clearing the sidewalk and the paths leading to the front door and garage.

Though tired, Lesley was unable to fall asleep without talking late into the night with Cass, and even then she slept badly. She had grown accustomed to the warm space of the Manhattan apartment; this house now seemed big and cold to her.

But today she was escaping, going back to New York on a well-heated train. She recollected the conversation she'd had with Dow last night. Only half-jokingly, he'd accused her of having a boyfriend in the City. He'd teased that Cass's phone number was a cover, because he had called twice and not gotten her, only a machine.

Forcing a laugh while her heart raced in fear, she had denied it, telling him that she and Cass were collaborating on an article for *Executive Educator* and were probably at the library.

She was, in fact, helping Cass to research and write a piece about values education.

The opening line read: "Heather has two mommies, and they both wonder why she can't read." Cass felt that the job of the overburdened public school system was to teach academics; not to advocate racial or sexual tolerance under the coalition of any umbrella, no matter how rainbow colored. Since there could be no uniformity of values in a city as diverse as New York, she said, the schools should not be expected to teach them. Values and respect should be taught by parents at home.

As a double minority, black and gay, Cass realized that the article would generate both personal and professional fallout, and so the work was going very slowly and carefully.

"Well, at least I wasn't lying," Lesley said, without much conviction, as she recounted Dow's comments to Cass later on.

"It's OK, pet," Cass reassured her. "I'm here, right beside you, whenever you're ready to tell them." She always said this whenever the subject of Lesley's children came up. She would have preferred to tell them and get it over, but things were going so well she didn't want to pressure Lesley.

Lesley complemented Cass's life, filling in the old hollows and plumping up her existence. Cass looked hard, very hard, for faults ¾ hairline cracks, even ¾ in this thing she was building with Lesley. She did not understand why it worked, but she was grateful that it did.

Cass had spent the last two years alone, wary of the risks that AIDS had imposed, even on her relatively low-risk community. She had also grown tired of the new politics of being gay and of the old stereotypes that still existed, even in the '90s. She had had many girlfriends, even those who considered themselves "femmes," for whom the kitchen was a highly charged area. They would remind her that they were professionals and not housewives and expect to be taken out to breakfast, lunch and dinner. More than once Cass had been forced to inquire, with biting sarcasm, how they had subsisted before they met her.

If they professed themselves liberated from the stove, she told them, they should also liberate themselves from the notion that the "man" ¾ and hence *she*¾ should always pay.

There was none of that baggage in this relationship; no gender politics. Maybe it was because Lesley had reared a family that she never

74

saw her domesticity in a demeaning light. She simply did things well and was as secure about her capabilities at home as she was about her work. It was one of the qualities Cass found most endearing about her. Unasked, unprompted, Lesley had assumed financial responsibility for the shopping and did most of the cooking, stating that she had to contribute, considering how much time she spent at Cass's place. With her there was never the question of bringing home the bacon *or* frying it up in the pan.

If pressed to cite a drawback to their relationship, Cass would say it was Lesley's excessive devotion to personal cleanliness. Any intimate advance would lead her, inevitably, to a quick trip "to freshen up first." This insecurity annoyed Cass, who found Lesley's personal smell ¾ a combination of *White Linen* and fabric softener ¾ comforting yet oddly exciting.

She suspected that this hang-up had been created in Lesley by Gene, and she privately cursed him for his ignorance. She was surprised and chagrined, therefore, when Lesley admitted that her over-sensitivity had been instilled by her mother, who had told her pubescent daughters that there was nothing more offensive than a dirty young woman. "Cleanliness is next to godliness," Mrs. Hillary had often lectured, embarrassing them and their father.

Cass offered silent thanks for her own enlightened ¾even clinical¾ parent. It was on the tip of her tongue to tell Lesley her mother was a silly bitch, but she didn't want to provoke a defense of Sister Hillary.

Instead, by word and deed, she tried to convince Lesley that her body was a temple and there was no place she would rather worship.

21

"Since it doesn't seem as if the snow's ever going to stop, we should go skiing, Cass. Why don't we visit my sister in Colorado?" Lesley suggested. Her hair in curlers, she looked hopefully over the top of her glasses. Their intimacy had progressed to the place where comfort sometimes took precedence over appearances at home.

"Not with *my* gay money!" Cass declared, looking up. "Actually, I was thinking more in terms of going home. I promised my mother I'd try to make it in February." She answered Lesley's questioning look with a tight smile. "Last year, when you left me.... Would you like to go?"

"Sure. Gene and I went with our friends years ago. We took a cruise from Miami to Bermuda and Mexico, Cozumel, I think."

"Oh," Cass said, "one of those *Caribbean* cruises. Well, would you like to visit the *West Indies,* now? Where I come from?"

"I'd love to go to the islands," Lesley agreed.

"Back up! Back up!" Cass snapped, not hiding her irritation. "We're going to Antigua. *One island!* The islands are not contiguous like the United States. I'm not from 'the islands' anymore than you're from 'North America.'"

She was on her soapbox again, and Lesley waited for the tirade to peter out. By now she was accustomed to Cass's Gemini temperament and knew when to take her irritation personally.

"It's disrespectful," Cass raged on. "*The islands.* Talking about people's countries as if they're merely some playground. Like Coney Island! Or Fantasy Island! Don't you-all realize that people have real lives down there? It's not just limbo and coconuts and rum, you know. And, personally, I don't know one person ¾not one¾ who says 'Yes mon!'"

Lesley simply said, "Then we'll go during winter recess."

Phoning her travel agent and even the contacts of contacts, Cass finally managed to book them on a flight to Antigua. This was quite a feat since it was high season, and every man, woman and child who could afford to was getting the hell out of New York. To leave on a Friday, they had to purchase first-class tickets at exorbitant prices, but excited at the thought of being somewhere warm, they wrote their checks gladly.

Cass waited until Lesley was not around to call her mother. Since they generally spoke every other weekend, Mrs. Shortman was momentarily panicked, thinking something terrible had happened.

"Everything's fine, Mother," Cass soothed. "I'm just calling to let you know that I definitely am coming home. And I'm bringing a friend."

"And that's what you're running up your phone bill to tell me?" her mother inquired, in exasperation. A sudden silence surged over the Atlantic. Then, "What kind of friend?"

"*You know*," Cass said. "I just wanted to prepare you, that's all."

"Prepare me for what?" her mother bristled. Their birthdays were only five days apart and they shared the same mercurial qualities. "What it is you're planning to do?"

"I'm not planning to do anything but have a nice holiday, OK. I thought I was being considerate, but, obviously, some people prefer to be surprised," Cass replied with some heat.

"Who you calling 'some people?'" Then, curiosity took over. In the years since her admission, Cass had never brought a woman home to meet her mother. Not even a platonic friend. More calmly now, Mrs. Shortman asked, "Who is she?"

"She's American," Cass answered. "Black. She has three children and ..."

"*Children?* What 'Nansi story you telling me?" her mother sputtered, confused. "Your friend is a married woman?"

"*Widow*, Mother, *widow*. Look, when I see you, I'll explain, all right." Cass sighed. "Anyway, just treat her nice when you meet her."

"The idea! As if I don't know how to behave!"

22

They did not bother to go to bed, since the flight was an early one and they were too wired to sleep. Cass recounted her coming-out story and told Lesley that Roma knew about their relationship.

"What about your father?" Lesley asked, looking worried.

"I really don't think he knows I'm gay," Cass replied slowly. "My mother said she'd tell him, but I don't believe she ever did; she probably thinks she's shielding him or something, or protecting me. And since that night, we've always avoided the subject. It might be different this time, though, when he sees you with me."

On the plane, next morning, Lesley insisted upon having a prep course on everyone she would meet in Antigua. Cass listed her cousins Fiona, Constance and Gregory, Luke and Dell, and Celeste, her parents' housekeeper.

"What are your parents like?"

"Mmm, typical parents. My mother nags my father, my father nags her, and Celeste nags both of them. The three of them are co-dependents," she laughed.

"And who's your favorite?"

"Oh God, I couldn't choose. My mother is my biggest fan, but my father...well, the man still calls me Fish, so that speaks for itself."

"How come you didn't get along with your grandmother?"

"Where'd you get that?"

"You told me she said you were spoiled rotten."

"*Please.* That was just rivalry between her and my mother. Granny couldn't wait for Mother to leave for work so she could pick up where she left off. Then when Celeste came, it was worse. You'll see what I mean when you get there. Sometimes I have to leave just to get some peace."

In an effort to distract Lesley, Cass went on to tell her about Luke and his wife, Dell.

Almost eight years ago, Cass related, her brother went home to watch an international cricket match and suddenly decided to stay. Well,

78

not so suddenly, actually. He had wanted to return home for years, a yearning that intensified when he lost his job as an aviation engineer during the period of airline deregulation.

Criticized by his wife for wanting to disrupt their teenage daughters' lives, Luke took a job with a cargo company at Newark Airport, hating the work and the commute. He lost weight and began to go gray, looking, as his father complained, "like a long streak of misery."

Unable to stand his son's obvious unhappiness, Drury bought Luke a ticket and persuaded him to go home for ten days of cricket and rejuvenation. Once he got there he simply stayed.

His wife, Cheryl, came from a respectable but poor family and did not remember the island with pleasure. She enjoyed the comfortable life the States afforded her and she also liked being able to help out her parents and siblings at home. She wanted to remain married to Luke, but preferably near a mall.

Luke did not contest the divorce and Cheryl got the house and custody of the girls.

Shortly after he determined that his marriage was over, Luke had taken up with Dell. His divorce was barely final when he announced his intention to marry her. Roma Shortman was horrified, sure that he was on the rebound and destined to repeat his mistake. But Luke was adamant that this was what he wanted to do.

Roma had never been crazy about Luke's first wife, but she could appreciate the appeal of her leggy beauty and effervescent personality. Dell, however, was thin, pale, and near-sighted. Though she would never admit to prejudice, Roma did not consider Dell (whom she distanced by calling Adele) in any way suited to her son.

The problem was really Dell's family. Her mother's name was Blythe, but the villagers had bastardized the pretty name and called her *Blight*. That she was of no consequence was apparent. Even children addressed her by her first name, not bothering to accord her the respect of "Miss," much less acknowledge her married status. And, indeed, her life seemed so blighted she simply accepted the disrespect.

Blythe was not from the village; she had moved there after her marriage. A slight, yellow-skinned girl with shy ways, she had a habit of looking down when she was spoken to. She could not engage her husband, and after the first year of marriage and while she was "big with child," he left her and returned to his previous and long-standing girlfriend.

Blythe was too humiliated to return to her aunt's house, which she had been so happy to leave. Her aunt had not approved of the marriage, anyway, and had refused to "keep up" the wedding. So Blythe stayed and bore the condescending pity of the village. Luckily, the little house in which she lived was owned by her husband and she did not have to pay rent. It also lacked electricity and running water, which she counted a blessing; she could keep expenses to a minimum.

That life was hard was putting it mildly. Small and pregnant, it was difficult for her to get work. The hotel nearby refused to hire her, and she was forced to ask for domestic jobs from those who could afford to pay; that's how she had come to the notice of Miss Gladys, Drury's mother. There usually was work to be found at the Shortman house because of all the grandchildren, and hiring Blythe was a help to Roma. When there wasn't much to do, Miss Gladys always had a meal for Blythe anyway.

Cass had been born only a few months earlier, and Roma had gotten a wealth of beautiful, well-made baby clothes from London. She was careful to save the things that Cass outgrew for the little woman who ate in their kitchen.

Blythe and her daughter were inseparable, simply because there was no one with whom she could leave the child while she washed and ironed in people's houses. Conspicuous only by the superior quality of her clothes, Dell learned early not to be a liability to her mother's tenuous existence; the child seldom cried. When she was old enough, Blythe would leave her at home surrounded by the books she picked up everywhere, with the injunction not to let anyone into the house under any circumstances. She need not have worried; Dell already distrusted most people.

Although Blythe could have gotten help ¾ many of the village men would have been happy to keep her ¾ she was not about to put some other woman in the position in which her own husband had placed her. Nor was she about to fall into the common trap of having another man's baby simply so that he could help her with the one she already had. So Blythe worked as hard as her little body could stand and prayed for deliverance from temptation.

When the older women would suggest she send Dell to ask her father's help, Blythe would give that shy smile and reply, "It ain't come to that yet."

In time the hotel did hire Blythe, and Celeste replaced her in the Shortman house. Now Blythe was able to provide better for her daughter, eventually sending Dell to board in town, where she attended a private high school. Blythe paid the old woman with whom Dell lived by cleaning the house and doing the laundry on her days off. Of course, Dell was old enough to do this, but her mother was determined to raise her to a different kind of life and encouraged her to stick to her books.

However, Dell never lost an opportunity to join the woman in the kitchen as she baked and decorated elaborate cakes for weddings, birthdays and christenings. In time, she became quite proficient and was able to take over the more complicated jobs.

After high school, Dell landed a well-paying job in one of the Canadian banks downtown and rose through the ranks. She possessed her mother's ability to squeeze five quarters out of every dollar, and after a few years she was able to build a nice house and persuade Blythe to retire from her maid's job.

But stress and overwork had taken their toll, and Blythe enjoyed barely a year of leisure and comfort. The old villagers swore that it was inactivity that had killed her and commented on the lovely casket in which she was to continue her unaccustomed rest.

It was no surprise that Dell had done well for herself and "looked after her mother good," they said. It was what they expected from a child lucky enough to have been the beneficiary of a good education, a good example, *and* her mother's canny ability to make something out of nothing. After the funeral, they wandered around her house and nodded to each other approvingly. With perfect understanding, Dell gravely accepted the compliments they offered in lieu of condolences.

Roma had heard about Dell's progress and was happy the lonely little girl had come up in the world. But she could not reconcile the charity baby she had known with the image of Dell as her daughter-in-law. Times had changed, she knew, and nowhere was that change more evident than in Antigua. Previously stratified by class and color, education and opportunities for advancement had leveled the playing field in the decades since the Shortmans had left the island. These days a cat could look at a king¾and did.

Drury was an affable man who lived to indulge his children. He was irritated by his wife's hand wringing and insisted that she leave Luke alone to enjoy his life.

Roma withdrew, visiting only when Luke and Dell's first child, Amaya Blythe, was born. Though Roma expressed pleasure in her grand-daughter and satisfaction that the marriage was going well, Dell insisted on treating her like a guest for the length of her stay.

Dell could recognize prejudice, no matter how heavily disguised or lightly expressed, and knew, despite Luke's protestations to the contrary, that Roma had not wanted her in the family. She would have been perfectly acceptable, say, as a childhood acquaintance of Cass, but not as Luke's wife.

Soon after, the Shortmans retired and returned home and, envious of the ease with which Drury fit into Luke's home life, Roma undertook the task of courting her daughter-in-law. During Dell's second pregnancy, Roma lavished her with attention, bringing her old nursing skills and new affection to bear. She even stopped calling her Adele.

Dell found it hard to resist this concentrated yet delicate assault, especially since her husband was so eager to see his wife and mother friends. With the birth of her son, she capitulated and Roma's heart finally took its ease.

"And they lived happily ever after," Lesley commented.

"I'm sure Dell wouldn't see her life as any fairy tale," Cass answered dryly. "She's a great person, very real, and she's made my brother happy. And my mother. You'll like their kids. Amaya is going on six now ¾a little old woman¾ and Lucas is almost four. My father was just ecstatic when Luke finally had a son, what with the three daughters already. Carrying on the Shortman name, you know, and all that macho crap."

"Did I ever tell you about my brother?"

Cass sat up and faced Lesley, surprised. "You have a brother?"

"Had. He was born between me and Lana, and he died when I was about two. That's when my mother practically lost her mind and joined the church."

"No shit!" Cass exclaimed.

"His name was Lennis. Most of the time I don't even remember him. In fact, I *don't* remember him, but Lana does. She told me about him, since my parents never talk about it."

"How'd he die?"

"Ran in front of my mother's car."

"Jesus! I'm sorry to hear that," Cass said slowly. "If that had happened to me, I think I'd have gone mad, too, pet." This certainly put Sister Hillary in a different light, she thought. "I always think of her as Sister Hillary. What's your mother's name, anyway?"

"Winsome."

"That's almost cruel. Although, in the literal sense, it's true. She's a fine-looking woman."

They both lapsed into silence for a while, then Cass slumped in her seat and pulled the blanket up to her chin. "Why don't we try to sleep until we get to Puerto Rico?" she suggested gently.

23

C ass was barely able to contain herself after they took off from San Juan, and when they finally sighted Antigua she grabbed Lesley's arm excitedly. She peered out the window with hungry eyes, and the plane had barely taxied to the terminal before she unsnapped her seat belt and grabbed the bag from overhead.

"Membership has it privileges," she quipped, smiling. "First class gets off first."

The February breeze was just hot enough, and they sighed appreciatively as they descended the steps and walked across the tarmac. Luckily, they were among the first on line in Immigration, as the building quickly and noisily filled up.

Lesley experienced a curious twinge as she watched Cass on the residents' line, laughing and talking with the official who was stamping her passport. The feeling persisted as her eyes followed Cass over to the luggage area where she greeted a redcap.

This is her turf, Lesley mused. In the ten minutes since we've been off the plane, she's become a different person. What was that twinge just now? Was it fear? Am I insecure because she is in a place that is so obviously hers and that I know nothing about? She rebuked herself for her feelings and forced a smile at the officer as he handed over her papers and wished her a pleasant stay.

Cass kept up her excited banter as they moved through Customs, telling the young officer that they were spending only a week and not to bother messing up their bags. He complied good naturedly, telling her he would take it out on Luke next time he came through.

"Yeah, do that," she said, grinning.

Around the doors, taxi drivers and resort reps clustered, waiting for the tourists whose dollars drove the economy. In the small group that was waiting for family members, it was easy to pick out Luke. Beaming, brother and sister approached each other and hugged, then Cass disengaged herself and introduced Lesley.

"Luke, this is Lesley. Lesley, Luke."

He ignored Lesley's outstretched hand and treated her to a hug. "Nice to be able to put a face to the name. Sorry, I'm a little sweaty," he apologized, plucking at his uniform shirt. "I started this morning at 4:00 and decided to just stick around and wait for the flight."

"Please," she dismissed his apology. "We've been up since then, too, and we're just as sticky." She surprised herself; she was not usually this familiar and forthcoming. It must be the unaccustomed heat, she decided.

"Anything you need to pick up in town before we leave?" Luke asked Cass, as they loaded the bags into his jeep.

"Nah, I'm not going into St. John's on a Friday afternoon," she said. "What I need is a shower."

From the backseat Lesley studied Luke. He looked much older than he did in the photos in Cass's apartment. He didn't have Marcus's bulk, which made him appear taller, and his sideburns and beard were heavily flecked with gray. But he was still a handsome man, and when he smiled, displaying the Shortman gap, he was downright sexy in an ascetic sort of way. She decided that Cass most resembled Luke, although she had no idea what the eldest brother might look like now. He and his sister were not close.

The landscape claimed her attention and she lost track of the conversation. Cass was right; it looked as though people had lives here and not merely like a tourist paradise. Houses of all sizes, designs and colors stood proudly or listed indifferently, and outside of people's yards, the place had an unstudied, untended beauty. No one had attempted to keep Nature in her place here, and palm trees, cactus and flowers grew at will, clustered in villages and coloring the stretches of open road. Herds of cows grazed inside paddocks, and sheep meandered along the pasturelands. Lending the landscape their own particular charm, old sugar mills recalled the colonial past. And everywhere, encircling, embracing, there were the hills.

But this was no bucolic backwater. The roads were lively with modern cars, mainly Japanese, and it seemed to Lesley that Luke honked his horn or flashed his lights to acknowledge every other driver. Everyone, it appeared, knew everyone else. Cass had told her that people recognized license plates just as readily as they did faces, and she understood now what she meant.

Slowing down, people called out to them, and more than once she watched Luke stick his head out the window to shout a message at another motorist or a pedestrian. The roads looked dangerously narrow and, to Lesley, they appeared to be driving on the wrong side of the road, but Cass had told her to expect this, too.

As they drove further into the country, Lesley saw more and more unoccupied land and marveled at the sense of space. She rejoined the conversation to inquire who owned the unoccupied acres.

"Government owns a lot of it," Luke answered, "and what's not cultivated belongs to people who are not ready to build yet. A lot of Antiguans who live away own land here, and when they're ready to retire they build homes and move down. People don't like to live on top of each other, and they buy big pieces of land so they can spread out."

Lesley was getting accustomed to the landscape and was commenting that she would love to own a place like the old estate house they had just passed atop an incline, when Luke slowed down and turned onto a rugged little road.

"Welcome to Montpelier, and welcome to my home," Cass said formally.

Around the corner, through a pair of spreading trees she would later learn were flamboyants, Lesley saw a big, square house, weathered to a soft yellow. Ficus all but camouflaged the low cement wall that fronted it, and the wrought iron gates looked like they hadn't been closed in years. The elbow of the porch was covered with with a feathery fern that provided both privacy and shade for the hammock that was slung there, and crotons and oleander skirted the front of the house. The sliding doors were open and curtains billowed out fatly. The place looked solid, comfortable and welcoming, and Lesley half-expected an old sheepdog to lope up and welcome them.

As they crunched to a stop, a buxom, middle-aged woman came out the front door. She turned around and shouted inside: "They reach!"

Leaving Luke to struggle with the bags, Cass and Lesley went up the shallow steps to the porch.

"How you-all so early?" the woman called out, a wide smile almost closing her eyes.

"When you travel first class, you get through early," Cass answered, laughing.

"Eh-eh, you move up, man," the woman retorted.

Cass bent and enveloped her in a huge hug and they rocked with pleasure for a moment. "Celeste, this is my friend, Lesley," she said finally. "Lesley, this is Celeste, my second mother."

Celeste beamed, extending her hand. "Nice to meet you, darlin'."

"Nice to meet you. I've heard so much about you," Lesley responded, her nervousness dissipating.

"Where's Mother and Daddy?" Cass inquired.

As though waiting for a cue, Roma Shortman bustled out the front door, laughing happily. She was a good-looking woman of medium height, sturdy, with glasses and a wealth of thick, graying hair, which clung damply to her temples.

"I was in the shower," she excused herself, chuckling. "We didn't expect you so early." She and Cass hugged, murmuring, their eyes closed, and she patted her daughter's back with obvious affection. Then she turned and surprised Lesley with a hug, too.

"Hello, Lesley," she said warmly, not waiting for Cass's introductions. "I'm Cass's mother. You had a nice flight?"

She smelled of Pond's, like her daughter, and Lesley responded to that and the familiarity of the gap-toothed smile. "Oh yes, I can see that. It's nice to meet you, too. The flight was lovely, thank you."

She was thrown off. Somehow she had expected, what? Not standoffishness, exactly, but at least reserve. They were greeting her like they had known her all their lives, or at least as if they were unaware of the situation. Everyone was being so normal.

"Let's go inside," Roma invited. "Luke, you can manage?"

"Where's Daddy?" Cass repeated, almost plaintively, as she grabbed a suitcase from her brother and gazed around.

"He's coming right back. He just went into the village to pick up ice. Electricity was off for the whole morning," Roma answered, bustling about. "But C'sandra, you look like you put on some weight, eh? Sit down by the window, Lesley, and catch the breeze. Give it a few minutes, and you'll cool off. Celeste, bring some lemonade, please.

"So, C'sandra," she said, finally seating herself, "how you leave everybody?"

"Everybody's fine. Cold, but fine. You should see the snow! Worse than '82! We couldn't wait to leave."

"Marcus write me?" Roma inquired sharply.

"I believe so. Sylvie gave me an envelope for you." Cass rummaged in her purse. "Here. Careful, there's money in it."

"Leave it for later," her mother chided, a litle selfconsciously, then turned to Lesley. "So, what you think of Antigua so far?" she inquired pleasantly.

They made animated conversation, with Celeste stepping in from the kitchen every few moments to offer comments or simply gaze at Cass. When they heard the crunch of tires, Cass leapt up and rushed out the front door.

"Daddy," they heard her exclaim.

"C'sandra!" a deep voice answered. "You beat me here, man. Lord, I long to see you. Hug me up, nuh."

Drury Shortman was an older version of Luke, tall and ascetic, his brown face and bald head polished by perspiration. To Lesley, he looked like Yul Brynner colored in mahogany. What a handsome man, she thought. His children resembled him in face, height and complexion, though Roma had contributed the signature smile.

He came over and greeted her warmly. "Lesley, nice to meet you, my dear. Nice to meet you. As long as you're C'sandra's friend," he said, "you're welcome here. They looking after you?"

As she relinquished his hand, Lesley saw Luke and Cass exchange small smiles. She suddenly found the situation funny and stifled a giggle.

About five-thirty, yet another car was heard outside, and Lesley rose to meet the person who fascinated her most. Dell had arrived with the two kids. The hugs and kisses, noise and laughter started again, and Lesley found herself experiencing another pang.

She identified it as envy. But not the mean-spirited, corrosive kind. Rather, she felt keenly the emptiness of her growing-up years, although their house had always been filled with church people; the emptiness that had been revived following Gene's death.

Lesley had always thought that gays had a hard life, slinking around on the edges of acceptance and forced to compensate with parades and ribbons and exclusive organizations. But it was she, straight as the proverbial arrow, who was poor by comparison, looking in with her nose pressed against the glass of Cass's convivial, embracing family life.

Just then, Celeste came in and asked everyone to come to the table; she had been holding dinner until Dell and the kids got there. By some chance, or maybe deliberately, Mr. Shortman came over and put his arm around Lesley in a fatherly way. "Come along, man; no shyness here. We're all family."

She willed her feelings away and smiled up at him. For this week at least, she was going to be a Shortman.

24

The week was going altogether too fast. Though Cass had said they would take things easy, that was hard to do. There were so many things to get done, so much to see. Declining Dell's offer to show Lesley around, Cass accepted the use of her car, instead, and played tour guide.

"I don't want to be mean, but Dell always drives likes she's anticipating a red light," Cass complained to Lesley, as she expertly backed the car out of the yard, "even out here, where there's no lights."

They went to the beach several times, cruised around the indented shoreline, and coasted through the rain forest. Lesley saw the public market at daybreak on Saturday; shook hands with the villagers who clustered around Cass after church at St. Philip's on Sunday morning; and danced atop Shirley Heights to steelband music that evening.

On Monday, they went to Miller's-by-the-Sea to meet James Matthias, the young man who had accompanied Cass to the prom and who was now a successful pediatrician, and his wife Jocelyn. Amused, Cass watched James's wife watch him, searching, perhaps, for signs of interest in Lesley. But after determining that Lesley was more than Cass's friend and, therefore, could hold no interest for her husband, she let down her guard. They had a good time drinking Wadadli beer, eating lobster, and enjoying the sand between their toes, as they watched the spectacular Caribbean sunset bleed into the sea.

It was easy to fall into the rhythms of everyday life. Since they had Dell's car, Lesley and Cass volunteered to pick up the kids after school and took them along on their jaunts, until Luke came to get them in the evening. On one occasion, Lesley found herself driving Celeste home to Bethesda, then stopping to buy bread at the little shop, as if she had done so every day of her life. It was impossible to feel like a stranger or to get lost.

On another day they went into St. John's to buy souvenirs for Lesley's coworkers and T-shirts for the boys, and Cass introduced her all around. Blacks, whites, Syrians, Lebanese, everybody seemed happy to see Cass, jokingly asking if she had lost her green card, inquiring about Marcus and Matthew, and sending messages to her parents.

"Do all these people know you're gay?" Lesley heard herself asking when they were alone for a moment.

"They never asked me," Cass answered dryly, "but I'm sure all the men suspect. In fact, I know they've inquired among themselves. If any of them has had me, I mean." She smiled wickedly. "Whoever should know has already been told. And now they've seen you with me, the others know, too."

They visited Fiona's job, spending almost an hour in her office. When she caught Lesley looking at her watch guiltily, Fiona was amused.

"Where you have to go?" she asked.

"Nowhere. It's just that we're keeping you from working," Lesley explained.

"You're not keeping me from anything," Fiona assured her. "You can't kill work, but work can certainly kill you. This is not New York; take it easy."

When they finally left, Fiona grabbed her purse and sauntered out with them, declaring that it was time for her lunch, anyway. So they walked up to Calypso, a delightful garden restaurant on Redcliffe Street, where they enjoyed a leisurely and convivial lunch.

Tonight, from where they sat on the verandah, Luke and Cass could catch the breezes that wafted down from the hills and cooled the flats. Cass thought she could smell ladies-of-the night, but wasn't sure if this was, indeed, their season. They could see clear to the airport, where runway lights dotted the distant darkness. Dell and Lesley's voices came to them from inside, and from a neighbor's television came the sounds of CNN Headline News.

"So," said Cass, inclining her chin toward the kitchen, "what do you think?"

"Of Lesley and Dell?" Luke smiled. "Or just Lesley?"

"Well, it's obvious that those two get on like a house on fire. What do you think of her? Her and me?"

"I like her. She smart. She nice looking. She can cook.... You and her, well, that's another story. No offense, Fish, but as far as I'm concerned, that woman ain't gay."

"So tell me something I don't know," Cass answered dryly. "You

90

don't think it can work?"

"Well, it's working now. She's not out and out with it, but anybody can see that she loves you, and not just in a buddy-buddy way. Though I see that, too. It's just that..."

"Just that what?"

"Well, since she isn't gay, what's going make her stay with you?"

"You're saying that, by myself, I'm not enough to make her stay?" Cass bristled, sitting up straight on the lounger. Her eyes glittered with anger.

"No, no, no!" he said hastily. "I'm not taking anything away from you, personally. But she's a woman who's been married, after all, Fish. She lived most of her life with a man. And I'm worried that if some man comes along who can offer her more, then she could very well leave. ..."

"In that case, you'd better watch Dell, then."

"What?" he asked, uncomprehendingly. "Dell?"

"Well, if some man comes along who's not prematurely gray, who doesn't have to spend half his salary to support two teenagers in the States, and who can afford to have her stay home with her children and just bake, as she would really love to do, then she could very well leave *you!*"

Luke was silent, thoughtful for two or three minutes as he compulsively smoothed his beard with his thumb and forefinger.

"Dell told you that?"

"Of course, Dell didn't tell me that! That's what *I'm* saying! If it's simply a matter of considering a better offer, why would *anybody* stay with anybody? You don't think that Dell loves you and the kids and your life together? And isn't that enough for her to stay?"

He nodded slowly. "When you put it like that, yes. I didn't mean to put you down, you know, Fish," he apologized. "I was just trying to say that there are certain things a woman gets accustomed to and ..."

"Like what, Luke? What is she accustomed to that I can't give her? What? A *dick?*"

He cleared his throat, again at a loss for words. Cass could be so damned blunt at times.

"I live in New York City, remember?" she asked softly. *"Babylon!* I can buy her any dick she wants. Any length, any thickness, any color,

91

with or without balls."

Luke looked at her serious face for a moment and then burst out laughing. "Yes, you can. And you would, too. OK, Fish. You win," he declared, throwing up his hands. "You have my blessing, if that's what you want."

"I want you to mean it," she said fiercely.

"I mean it. God above me," he swore, crossing his fingers and raising them to his lips like they had done as children.

25

They drove slowly, with the sun-roof open to the warm night air. They had enjoyed themselves and were picking over the evening.

"Lesley," Cass said suddenly, "could you live down here?"

"I get the feeling this isn't a casual question."

"Your feeling's right."

"Why'd you ask?"

She sighed. "I've spent nearly thirty years in New York and I'm tired of it: the rat race, the crime, the cold, the mayor, the Board of Ed. Just *tired!* And I always planned to come home after I retire ¾ which is only three years away now, thank God. I really need the break.

"Life is so simple here, pet." She shook her head, as if amazed. "You don't have to worry about the homophobes; people are amused, more than anything else, to hear you're gay. They'll tell you it's because you haven't met the right man yet, or you need to be screwed right, or some such crap. They'll talk about you, for sure, but they certainly won't hurt you.

"You don't have to think about race and color all the time, either; you're just a person, you know. You go about your business, and after work, you're home in twenty minutes. No matter where you live, you can be on the beach ten minutes after that. It's free and you can always find a place to park. I'm ready for this kind of life."

She sighed heavily. "I want to be here for my parents, too. They're getting old, and they need somebody. Not to look after them, of course; my parents wouldn't tolerate it. But just to call them every day. Make them dinner on Sundays. Dell does her best, but she has two small kids after all.

"And I want to watch Amaya grow up. I mean, Lucas doesn't even remember me, and by the time he gets to know me again, poor thing, I'll be gone," she said shakily.

Lesley feared that Cass was going to cry. She knew exactly how Cass felt; that feeling of wanting to belong to something larger than yourself. Maybe that's why they were such kindred spirits.

"I've made inquiries at the college here about a teaching position," Cass went on, "and it looks promising. So I'd have a job to come to. And I have some money saved, in addition to my pension, so I could live pretty well. Probably better than I do in New York."

The car was crawling now. "But I don't want to leave without you."

Lesley gazed out the window at the dark pastureland. She knew it was coming and was flattered that Cass should feel this way; she was touched, really. But how would the kids feel about her being so far away? They were grown, but they still needed her....

Cass had her parents, her brother and his family, and her friends; in time she would forget. But I won't forget her, she admitted.

What did she have by herself in New York? An empty house to rattle around in. Her job, if that lasted much longer. Visits from the boys every few Sundays. She remembered how she had felt when she walked out on Cass last year: alone, unconnected, unloving, unloved. No, Antigua wasn't that far; no farther than the West Coast, really.

"Would I need something like a green card to work here?"

"You'll come?" Cass asked tentatively, trying to quash her rising hope.

"I don't think I want to be in New York without you either, Cass," she said simply.

Cass screamed incredulously, delightedly. "I was afraid you'd tell me you couldn't leave the kids. A green card? As far as I'm concerned, you don't even have to work. Or you and Dell can open a catering business or something. You can cook, she can bake." Cass couldn't stop laughing. "She'd love that!"

"You're right. I could buy an industrial stove and a couple freezers, and I have a million gadgets already. Dell's got a lot, too." The excitement was catching. "I'll bring down the car, and we can get a little house..."

"I already have a house. The house belongs to me, didn't you know?"

"No, I didn't. Since when?"

"Years ago. My parents figured since I didn't have a husband, they'd make sure I had someplace to live."

"But I thought your father didn't know."

"Yeah, but my mother convinced him I was going to be a pitiful old maid begging my brothers' wives for charity."

"That's flattering. I think my parents are leaving us their house jointly."

"My brother Matthew thought so, too. I had told Luke about it, of course, and I assumed my parents would tell the other two. But when Granny died and we came home for the funeral, there was this huge scene."

Although it was almost eleven years ago, Cass recalled the showdown clearly. The day after the funeral, Matthew had asked his mother what would become of the house now that his grandmother was gone. They could get good rent for it, he said, and within a few years, that money could finance a second house.

"You thinking far-far," was Roma's cryptic answer.

"Yes. I'm going run it by Daddy and hear what he thinks."

"Is really up to C'sandra," she said levelly. "We going leave the house to her."

Matthew looked at his mother as though he had never seen her before.

"You going do what?"

"We going leave the house to her," Roma enunciated carefully.

"What *she* do that you going give her a whole house?" he asked, glaring at Cass who sat staring out the window.

"What *you* do for us to send you to law school?"

Roma couldn't believe a son of hers could be so *grudgeful*. Especially of his own sister. As if he ever planned to move back here!

"Look, Granny wouldn't want things to go like this," Matthew said, trying a different approach. "Why don't you sell the house and split it between everybody, then?"

"When last you see Granny to know what she would want? Is Cassandra and Luke she been seeing all these years. Even Marcus would send to her now and then. What she ever get from you but a card Christmastime?" Roma's voice was rising and Celeste came to stand defensively in the doorway of the dining room.

"Listen, we gave Marcus and Luke the down payment for their houses," she went on flatly. "You have yours. This is ours, and we say it belongs to C'sandra."

Matthew turned on Cass accusingly. "That's why you run down here every opportunity you get, eh? You know you don't have to save your money for any mortgage," he said scathingly. "It seems like all you have to do to get property around here is turn anti-man!"

The hand is faster than the eye. No one had seen Roma's hand flash out, but they all heard the echo of the slap.

Jumping up, Matthew overturned the chair and bawled at his mother like a wounded animal. "Don't hit me, man! Is true! You know is true!"

Roma balled her hand into a fist this time and Celeste and Cass sprang to stop her. Drury rushed into the room, angry that no one seemed to be respecting the memory of his just-buried mother.

"What the hell going on?" he demanded. "Roma, what happen? Celeste?"

"Nothing happen, Mr. Dru," Celeste answered, staring malevolently at Matthew. From a boy, this one had been proud and pushy. Forward, too, talking to Miss Roma like that!

"What you mean nothing happen? Matthew?"

"Not a thing, Daddy," he answered, walking out of the room. "Not a thing."

Matthew left the next day without saying goodbye to any of the women in the house.

"And you haven't spoken since?" Lesley inquired, shocked.

"Oh, yes. Marcus talked to him when he got back to New York, and eventually he called and apologized to Mother. But it wasn't the same after that. They would come for Thanksgiving or Christmas, but it was like having guests, you know, not family, even though his wife tried hard. Since my parents moved back, I only see him at Marcus and Sylvie's."

"What happened to the house before your parents moved back?"

"We rented it and left Celeste in charge. But I paid the taxes and maintained it. That way, I felt like the house was really mine."

"Are we going to live with your parents when we move down?"

"They'd probably prefer to move to the other house. It's closer to town and more modern. Anyway, we don't have to settle this right now. We have a couple years to plan."

"This might be a bit forward, but how did your parents make all their money?"

"You mean other than the fact that we went to public school and CUNY and lived at home till we were 25?" Cass laughed.

"My parents are very shrewd people. They enjoy their comforts but they believe in saving, too," Cass said, admiringly. "Daddy inherited the house from my grandmother, so my parents never had a mortgage here, and they were able to migrate with a good amount of money.

"Even so, they always worked hard: Mother would do a little private nursing on the side, you know, and Daddy did well selling insurance to other West Indians over the years. When we started working, we had to contribute to the house, too. Except for Matthew. After undergrad, he went to law school and never lived at home again. But my parents never touched that money; they gave it back to us when we needed it. Like when the boys bought their houses. And they helped me buy my first car. I guess, in essence, we lived at home for free....

"Anyway, when they were ready to come back here, they sold their house in Queens and built a small one on my mother's land in Fitches Creek; that's on the other side of the airport. But since I wasn't ready to come home, I thought it was better for them to live at Montpelier and rent the new house. Make some of their money back, you know. So they did that."

"Gene was like that, too," Leslie nodded approvingly. "Very smart. When he left the service, he took advantage of every concession the government made to veterans, whether it was student loans or mortgages. I can't tell you how much it helped us."

They were pulling into the gate by this time, and Cass had barely turned off the ignition before they saw the lights come on.

"C'sandra," Mrs. Shortman called out as the front door opened, "that's you?"

"How many people you giving keys to, Mother?" Cass joked.

"I thought you said you were spending the night," Roma chided, squinting in the lights. Her robe was on the wrong side, but neither of them bothered to tell her.

"I lied," Cass answered, laughing. "I didn't want you waiting up."

"You want something to eat, dear?" Roma inquired of Lesley. "Celeste made some lovely split-pea soup. I can heat it up for you."

"We're coming from Dell's, Mother. How could we be hungry?" Cass asked. "She sent you a bread pudding."

"You want a slice with some tea then?"

"Nah, too hot for that. We're going to bed now."

"All right, all right," she said, moving back toward her bedroom. "I'll see you in the morning then. Sleep good."

26

On their last evening, after they had made their goodbyes in town, Cass took Lesley to Le Bistro, her favorite restaurant. The lamb was exquisite and the service excellent, but both were a little melancholy, knowing that all too soon, they would be back in the city they had been so happy to leave.

"Ready?" Cass asked Lesley, as she finished her cognac. "I have a goodbye present for you."

They drove a short distance south to Jabberwock Beach, where Cass parked as close to the water as she could safely get and lowered the windows.

The moon, huge and white, painted a path on the surface of the black water and softly illuminated the interior of the car. The slap of the waves hitting the sand at high tide was regular, rhythmic, and the salty air gently lifted Lesley's hair and infiltrated her dress.

In tune with the Van Gogh beauty of the night, Cass took Lesley's hand, stroking it as they looked dreamily over the dark sea. "And I would be the moon," she recited, invoking Audre Lorde, "spoken over your beckoning flesh, breaking against reservations, beaching thought, my hands at your high tide, over and under inside you, and the passing of hunger, attended, forgotten."

Lesley slid over the seat to rest her head against Cass's shoulder, like it was the most natural thing in the world. And when Cass turned to raise Lesley's face and press her lips, that, too, was only logical.

Neither felt particularly sexual. Rather, they felt¾more than they ever had before¾a connection that transcended physical desire and entered the realm of the spiritual. At that moment, each woman knew there was no place she'd rather be, no person she'd rather be with. Seamlessly, they were one. And chastely, they kissed again.

"If ever I ask myself why," Lesley thought, "I will remember tonight."

As they were driving into the yard, the drizzle that had begun on the way home became heavier. They dashed onto the porch and let themselves in silently.

Stuffing the clothes she had just taken off into her suitcase, Lesley was startled to see Cass appear in her doorway. Startled, because on the night of their arrival, an amused Cass had confided that Roma had charged her to "respect the house." Their rooms were separated from each other only by the large, old-fashioned bathroom and from Cass's parents by the whole width of the house, but they had behaved with the strictest propriety.

"What're you doing?" Lesley whispered, as Cass gently closed the door and got into the bed.

"It's raining," she answered, a satisfied look on her face. "Listen to it on the roof. You don't hear this in a New York high-rise."

Lesley was still tentative and remained standing with a slight frown on her face.

"Relax," Cass urged. "Just lie down and listen. Where's your sense of romance?"

The last thing Lesley wanted was to betray the trust of the woman who had accepted her without the quirk of an eyebrow.

"Your mother!" she protested.

"Are you cursing at me?" Cass laughed. Then seriously, "My mother would never come in here, pet. Don't worry, we're not going to do anything." She patted the pillow invitingly. "Come."

Slipping in next to her lover, Lesley gradually allowed her misgivings to fade and, inevitably, their bodies conformed to their usual pattern.

The rain was, indeed, seductive, and through the open window they could see it, like a curtain of quicksilver, and smell its earthy sensuality.

They didn't talk, just cuddled and enjoyed the warmth they created under the cool sheets.

"Thanks for sharing your moon with me, Cass," Lesley murmured drowsily.

"Our moon, pet." She reached back to pat Lesley's thigh. "It's our moon, now."

27

The phone was ringing as Cass entered the apartment. "Hello," she answered, still breathing shallowly from the cold.

"Miss Shortman?"

It was Seth. She was not surprised to hear from him, since they had had several conversations about finding him a position after graduation. She had worked her contacts like an incumbent during election week and his prospects were good.

"Hi, guy! What's up?" Cass greeted him gaily. "I spoke to Ms. Schapiro today and we have a meeting set for Tuesday afternoon. That's good for you?"

"Thanks, Miss Shortman. That's fine." He sounded subdued.

"You OK? Your mom's not here right now."

"I know. Actually, I wanted to talk to you."

"Shoot."

She was colder when she hung up than she was when she came in, and she was glad she was still wearing her old shearling. According to Seth, his girlfriend Yoline was more than three months pregnant. She had been scared to tell him until a week ago, he said. Since then, Seth had not known how to bring it up to Cass, for professional reasons, or to his mother, for obvious reasons. He was worried about how she would take the news.

Cass kicked off her boots and sank down onto the couch, pulling the blanket that lay there around her. She was a little crushed, because her hopes for Seth had been so high, her enthusiasm so great. But though disappointed, Cass was not angry at him. Instead, some sixth sense ¾ or was she grasping at straws ¾ was persuading her that it was not an accident, as he explained it, but a deliberate act on Yoline's part.

Her mind went back to Christmas Day, and she recalled her first and subsequent impressions of Yoline Bonnick. Cass reexamined every piece of information that Lesley had ever volunteered about the relationship. Yoline was almost two years older than Seth. Her father had died during her sophomore year, leaving his wife and Yoline to bring up the two much-younger boys. She had been Seth's mentor during his freshman year and they had started dating. Financial problems had forced her to drop out and get a full-time job to help her mother, but the relationship had continued, since Seth shared an apartment not far from her family. They had been going out for more than three years.

Cass had liked the girl. She was sweet, though she hadn't struck her as particularly smart. In fact, Dow had gently poked fun at her all day, making jokes that seemed to go over her head. Cass had found her a little insecure and was amused at her efforts to be one of the family, bustling about helping Lesley and trying to anticipate Generes's needs. It was obvious she loved Seth, and he loved her, too, Cass admitted, but to do this? What was she afraid of? That he would graduate and leave her when he moved from the neighborhood?

How was she going to break this news to Lesley, as she had promised Seth? She worried about it as she dragged herself into the bedroom and changed her clothes, then began supper. Lesley had two meetings and would be exhausted and hungry when she came in. It was Tuesday, and Cass decided to wait until Friday night to tell her. What was the harm? Yoline couldn't get anymore pregnant than she already was. And however badly Lesley took it, at least she would have two days to deal with it before having to go back to work.

Resolved, Cass abandoned her plans for a simple pasta salad and popped two salmon steaks into the microwave to defrost. She had time to make her a nice dinner. There was even some wine in the refrigerator. They would eat and after they showered, she would give Lesley a nice massage. If she felt up to it, maybe they would even make love.

28

Cass strained to keep things as normal as possible and was surprised on Friday morning when Lesley asked, with concern in her tone, if she was all right. Cass shrugged off her inquiry, murmuring something about the damn snow, which had yet to melt.

Late that evening, she stared blankly at the television while Lesley, facing the bottom of the bed, turned the pages of one of Cass's books, something about the Princess of Wales. Cass knew she was really not reading; she wanted to make love. Lesley never came right out and said so; rather she intimated that she was in the mood by her choice of pajamas and her body language.

"Pet?"

"Mmm?"

"I have to talk to you."

Lesley immediately turned over, eyes wide, heart thudding in fear. She knew something was wrong; had known it for days. She sat up slowly and braced herself.

"So, talk to me."

Cass's carefully rehearsed speech deserted her. Lesley was too wary, too suspicious. She stammered. "Well, something's come up, and I don't want you to get upset."

"You're leaving me? Is that why you've been walking on tiptoe all week?" Lesley demanded accusingly. She was already berating herself for the way she was dressed and feeling like a cheap fool. Here she was thinking of sex, and Cass was probably thinking about someone else.

"Hey, hey, *hey!* Who said anything about leaving?" Cass took Lesley by the shoulders. "This isn't about us. It's about Seth."

Lesley sagged against Cass. "Oh," was all she could say for a long moment. Then with relief, "He didn't get the position in 29?"

"We'll know about that next Tuesday. Actually, he called a few days ago to talk," Cass admitted. Plunging on, she announced, "Yoline's pregnant. Three months gone. He found out last week and he didn't know how to tell you, and I said I would: Yoline's pregnant."

Lesley just looked at her. She understood, but she didn't know what to say. She was a bit surprised, too. Sure, she had assumed Seth was sexually active. For God's sake, he was 22 years old. But it really was the last thing she expected from him.

Lesley wondered why Seth would confide in Cass, but she was controlled enough not to wonder aloud, knowing the query would hurt. For a moment, she wondered if *her* feelings should be hurt.

Cass was staring at her now, and she knew she should say something.

"When are they getting married?" she asked faintly.

"Married?" Cass hadn't even considered that.

"They're not planning to get married?"

"Were they planning to before?" Cass countered.

"No, but things have changed, wouldn't you say?"

"No," Cass stated bluntly.

"What do you mean 'no'? What did her mother say?"

"Lesley, I don't know what her mother said. Your son was concerned about how *you* would feel. He didn't get into Mrs. Bonnick, and I didn't ask."

"I guess I'll have to call her then."

"Call her and say what?"

"I don't know. Tell her I'm sorry and ..."

"Sorry for what?" Cass interjected. "Last I heard, Yoline was 23 years old. You think she didn't know what she was doing?"

Lesley bristled. "And *what* was she doing, Cass?"

"Nothing about this strikes you as suspicious?" Cass asked, peering at her closely. "They're going out for three years and nothing happens. He's getting ready to graduate, move out of her neighborhood and go off to France, and, all of a sudden, she's pregnant and too scared to tell him until it's too late! Scared of Seth? Gimme a break."

"I'm sure that girl was scared and confused, keeping the news to herself all this time," Lesley said sharply.

"And Seth isn't? You haven't even asked how he is, Lesley. You wouldn't do that if it were Dow!"

Lesley's jaw hardened. "I resent that!"

"Resent it all you want; it's true, though." Cass refused to back down. "Seth is barely 22 and just getting out of school, and you're not even thinking about how this could affect his life."

"I am!"

"The kid was so excited about getting a job. It's a damn shame!"

"Well, the girl didn't make this baby by herself."

"No, but she *planned* it by herself, I'll bet."

"So what do you suggest, Cass?" The weight of her sarcasm made her lips curl. "He should just let her go through this by herself? Just make her the talk of her family and friends?"

"This is 1994, Lesley Gorton! What the hell are you talking about?" Cass was astounded.

Suddenly, the clouds parted and Cass understood. She remembered their first conversation at the hotel. This wasn't about Yoline and Seth; this was about Lesley and Gene. Lesley assumed that Yoline was the "victim" of Seth's "accident," as she had been with Gene, and she was projecting her feelings onto the girl.

Lesley had had to fumblingly, embarrassedly, explain to her parents what had happened, and she remembered her mother's reaction¾or the lack of it. Mrs. Hillary had never comforted her, never inquired how her frightened daughter might have felt. Like Job, she simply accepted it as one of the trials that God had sent to test her.

Meanwhile Gene's parents were sure she had "done it" on purpose to trap him. It never occurred to them that being left pregnant and alone, not knowing in what condition he would return, or *if* he would return from Vietnam, was not an attractive proposition.

It wasn't that she didn't care about Seth, Cass realized; her empathy simply lay with Yoline. Cass calmed down and took Lesley's clenched hand.

"Listen, pet, this isn't about you," she said gently. "Yoline isn't you. The circumstances are different, entirely different. Don't confuse Seth with Gene, either."

"Gene was a good man," Lesley defended automatically.

"And Seth's a good kid. A responsible boy. Yoline was on the pill, Lesley; he wasn't taking chances. I think you need to think about Seth for a change."

That would be a change, Lesley admitted to herself. Generally, she didn't *really* think about Seth because he never gave her cause to think about him. Although he was the youngest, he had never been a brat. Seth was the child she had counted on to be quiet, to entertain himself, to behave. She had never *ignored* him; he simply had not required much. He wasn't demanding and moody like the other two, and had been placid and accommodating, even as a baby. Now her baby was going to have a baby.

My word, she was going to be a grandmother!

Wearily, she squeezed Cass's hand. "What do you suggest?" she asked again. This time the inflection was different. The realities of what Cass had said were sinking in.

"First of all, I think you should *ask* Seth what he wants to do. Maybe they *don't* want to get married. Not everyone does, you know," Cass said reasonably. "And if they want to, well, they want to. She has a job, and Seth will be working by the time the baby gets here.

"I know babies are expensive, but I don't see any reason why he shouldn't go on to grad school. Columbia has a minority program for math and science teachers. Queens College, too. I know he would qualify. The only thing that could stop him is Yoline herself, how supportive she would be. And God knows she *should* be!" Cass could not resist that dig.

Lesley ignored it. "Do you think I should offer them the house?"

"Could they afford it?"

"It's paid for, but I guess running a house might be too much with a new baby."

"Why don't you call him?"

"Yeah, give me the phone."

Handing her the phone, Cass relinquished Lesley's hand and left the room, closing the door behind her.

Lesley held the phone for a while before she dialed. She didn't quite know what to say, and the realization made her sad¾because she always knew how to accommodate and placate Dow and Generes. She always had the words.

"Seth, it's Mommy. How are you feeling, hon?"

"You talked to Miss Shortman, Mom?"

"Yes, but I wanted to hear it from you."

He was relieved that she had called and even more grateful that she was not angry. Over the years, he had listened to her admonishments to Generes and Dow, but nobody ever expected that it would be Seth who would prematurely start a family.

He insisted that he had been careful and that Yoline was on the pill. He couldn't understand why she hadn't told him at once, he said. And Lesley, with Cass's conviction at the front of her mind, simply murmured sympathetically.

Seth wanted to marry Yoline, and his mother was proud of his decision to do so and go ahead with school. Having been through it all herself, she would not want him to do less. They would have a simple civil ceremony, he said, with a small reception after. He assured her he would pay for it.

"What about France?" she inquired.

"I don't think I can afford that now," he answered ruefully.

"Of course you can. That's your graduation gift."

"Yeah, but I'll need the spending money to pay for the wedding."

"Listen, Seth," Lesley said, suddenly firm, "you're going. You'll be working full time in September and going to grad school, and trust me, the time will never come again. *You're going.*"

"Mom, I can't afford it," he protested.

"I've still got some insurance money left... When do you plan to have the wedding anyway?"

"Well, Yoline wants to do it right away, before she starts showing."

Lesley felt chilled. Cass may have been right after all. But she wasn't going to start things off by running down Seth's future wife. She used to like Yoline and she would try to concentrate on the good things about her.

"I'll call her and Mrs. Bonnick in the morning. It's kinda late now. Her mother does know, doesn't she?"

"She knew before me."

"She did, huh? Listen, hon, call your brother and ask him to come home tomorrow. We have a lot to talk about. Meet me at home about midday, OK."

"Bring Miss Shortman, too, Mom. I owe her."

Lesley put the phone down and went out to sit on the couch with Cass.

"I think you're right, Cass," she said quietly. "I just hope that things work out. For both of them."

"I hope so, too."

29

The ride out to the Island was quiet, as Lesley was absorbed in her own thoughts and speculations. Seth met them at the station. Cass looked at him closely. Did he look a little older, or was she imagining things that weren't there? He kissed his mother and hugged Cass tightly, whispering his thanks.

The mood, as they entered the house, was almost funereal and the scowl on Dow's face didn't lighten the atmosphere. He greeted his mother and Cass politely enough, but was almost hostile toward his brother.

To buy time, perhaps, Lesley bustled about the kitchen making sandwiches and heating cans of soup. When they sat around the table, however, nobody appeared to have much of an appetite. Cass was actually hungry, but she felt her usual hearty appreciation for anything Lesley made was out of place at this time.

"I don't mind telling you, Mom, that I'm pissed, just *pissed*," Dow finally announced.

"I hear you, Dow," Lesley responded placatingly, "but this is about Seth, OK."

"You know she did it on purpose, don't you?" Dow was not to be stopped.

"Did what on purpose?" Seth turned on him angrily, taking both women by surprise.

"Got herself knocked up. I saw it coming. And I even warned you,

you damn fool!"

"Dow!" Lesley cut in. "Take it easy, OK. We're here to talk. Relax, just relax."

"It's all over, Mom. Wait, you'll see. As soon as Yoline has this one, boom, another one will be on the way," Dow continued.

"That's not true," Seth contradicted. "We're gonna wait a while."

"We're gonna wait a while," Dow mocked. "Like *you'll* get to have a say. Yoline and her old lady have got you bagged. Bagged!"

"Dow! Please!" Lesley threw her hands up. "Seth, when, exactly, are you planning to do this thing?"

"Sometime next month, Yoline said."

"Yoline said," Dow taunted.

Abruptly, Seth jumped up and shoved Dow, and he and the chair toppled over. Before Lesley or Cass could stop them, they were grappling with each other, and Seth had Dow by the throat jammed up against the refrigerator. Cass, who was closer, grabbed Seth by the belt trying to drag him off his brother, while Lesley screamed at them to stop.

His face turning red, Dow hammered at his brother's face and chest. The fridge rocked with his struggles as he tried to get away from Seth's grip. In desperation, Lesley grabbed the tureen of soup and threw it at the boys, splashing Cass in the process. All three suddenly stopped and turned to look at Lesley.

"Shit!" Cass spluttered, glad she was wearing jeans. She had never seen Lesley like this.

"Stop it!" Lesley was screaming. "What's wrong with the two of you? Just stop it, I said. Seth, let him go. Dow, leave him alone. We're here to talk. *Talk!* And if you start again, I'll choke both of you, myself."

Cass busily handed paper towels to both of them and went to the broom closet and got the mop.

The brothers eyed each other warily, as Lesley got her date book and began to make plans. Who would have thought this was how the first wedding in the family would begin?

"I want you to be my witness, Dow," Seth said to his brother levelly, not pleading.

"Fine," Dow answered. Seth could not understand the level of hurt he was feeling. Hell, he didn't understand it himself. All he understood was that Seth was a fine young man, yet his life was going the way of most of the decent brothers Dow knew¾downhill. But what was done was done, he forced himself to acknowledge, and he, like Seth, would just have to deal with it. He wondered, however, if their relationship could rebound from this blow.

"Mrs. Bonnick said we could have the basement," Seth was saying. "It's self-contained, you know."

"What?" Dow heard himself shouting again. "You're gonna live there, too?"

"I don't think that's a good idea, Seth." Cass abandoned her resolve not to get involved. "You two should really start your life on your own."

Lesley nodded in agreement. "Why would you want to do that, hon?" she asked.

"Well, her mother kinda depends on her for help, financially, and it would be hard on them if Yoline left now," he explained. "It wouldn't be forever."

"Let her *rent* the damn basement then!" Dow ground out. "That's what she should do."

"Did you already tell her yes?" Lesley inquired.

"No, Yoline brought it up earlier today. She said her mother could help out with the baby, you know. And I figured it would be a break for her when I'm at school... ." He shrugged helplessly, and they all realized for the first time that Seth, too, was under pressure, more pressure than any of them. He was just a kid trying to assume a man's responsibilities, and Lesley wanted to weep for her son.

"Let's take it one step at a time, Seth," she said gently and reasonably. "The baby won't be here until, when, September? Marriage isn't like dating, you know. You and Yoline will need time to yourselves, to get to know each other. Your brother is right. Let Mrs. Bonnick rent her basement if she needs the money. You two shouldn't tie your future to her finances.

"Get an apartment. I'm sure you can find something affordable in Queens, close to your job. And when the baby comes and Yoline needs help, you'll get a babysitter, like everybody else. I'll help you, and Mrs. Bonnick will too. She's not going to turn her back on her grandchild just because it doesn't live on the premises."

"If it's a boy, maybe I'll let you name him," Seth joked to his brother.

Dow forced a smile; Seth was trying to be conciliatory. "Deal. But, if it's a girl, do me a favor: Don't let Generes name her."

"You got that right," he answered.

After the boys went up to their room, Lesley called Mrs. Bonnick. Cass cautioned her, no matter what Yoline's mother said, not to apologize. She sat at the kitchen table, legs crossed and arms folded, keeping a watchful eye and keen ear on Lesley's conversation.

"Myrlie, hi, it's Lesley. How are you? I'm sor...." Cass's eyebrows practically disappeared into her hairline. "Well, I didn't call because I only heard about it last night."

Myrlie Bonnick had already composed a recital of reasons why Seth should not "spoil" her daughter and ruin her future. She complained that Seth would be "riding up and down France" after graduation, leaving her Yoline all alone. She was hostile and defensive, assuming that Lesley would be angry and opposed to the marriage. But Lesley's calm agreement took the wind out of her sails, and deflated, she was finally ready to discuss the upcoming nuptials.

Although she would have preferred a church wedding, Mrs. Bonnick said, there was no time for banns to be called, so a civil ceremony would have to do. Unfortunately, she continued, her relatives in Panama would not be able to come at such short notice, either, therefore a small reception at her house would suffice. About 25 people on her side, she said. Could she have Lesley's list of guests as soon as possible, please? The woman was actually excited at the prospect of her daughter's marriage; the acrid smell of gunpowder did not faze her.

The conversation lasted more than an hour as the two mothers worked out details. Yoline and Seth would get married on the second Friday in April, and there would be a reception the following day at Mrs. Bonnick's house. The Bonnicks would pay for the party. After the wedding, the couple would stay in Yoline's mother's basement until Seth returned from his trip, and the Gortons would stand the expense of setting them up in their own place after that.

It was settled: Seth would become a husband, college graduate, teacher and father¾in that order ¾ all within six months.

That night Lesley lay upstairs, her hands folded behind her head.

She wondered what Gene would have thought, how he would have advised his son. Would he have been angry with Seth for complicating his young life, or sympathetic about what had happened, using himself as an example to show that things could work out all right? Maybe he simply would have been delighted to become a grandfather, regardless of the circumstances.

For the first time, she allowed her thoughts to wander boldly down a road they had always skirted before: Had she not gotten pregnant, would she have married Gene, who was, initially, her sister's friend? There had been hundreds of eligible young men during her college years, and she had gotten to know a few of them. Had she made the wrong decision? She had not offered any opposition to Gene's suggestion that they get married before he went off to Vietnam. Suppose she had?

Foolish thought. At that time, 1968, a young, pregnant girl didn't have the choices available now. People simply did the decent thing and got married. She wasn't being fair, Lesley chided herself. She had liked Gene well enough. He had been kind, faithful, a good provider. He had loved her and they'd had a good marriage.

Was this how it would be for her son? Would Seth settle down with Yoline thinking that this was life and he must make the best of it? She felt sad that his possibilities would be so summarily circumscribed and pledged to help him get to wherever it was he dreamed of going. Not as her own mother had helped her ¾ out of a sense of duty. She would help her son out of love. And, since she was being so honest with herself, out of a sense of guilt for what could only be called benign neglect. He was such a good kid; no wonder Yoline wanted to keep him.

Lesley ached for Cass's presence. Cass would comfort and persuade her that this marriage would work. Each minute seemed to stretch past its usual span as Lesley counted sheep, then thought of names for her grandchild. Finally, she got up and walked softly down the hall toward the bathroom. Switching on the light, she rummaged in the medicine cabinet, searching for the sleeping pills she used to take after Gene's death.

The door opened and closed and, suddenly, Cass was in the room. Unable to sleep, herself, Cass had heard Lesley's light footsteps go down the hall and, instinctively, followed her. Wordlessly, she pulled Lesley into her arms and held her close as they leaned against the door. Relief flooded Lesley, and hot tears streamed down her face as she cried for her little boy, suddenly turned man, and for her own fears.

Assuaging her woman's pain, Cass defied the presence of the men of the house, both alive and dead.

30

This was the second in three weekends that Cass was spending in Generes's room. She was beginning to understand the dynamics of being not simply a girlfriend but a member of the family. She had never had the experience of being responsible for anyone before.

Not that she was really responsible, in the strictest sense of the word, for Lesley's well-being. But after Lesley had provided support for Seth, tended to the emotional needs of Dow, negotiated with Mrs. Bonnick, and delicately explained the rush of the wedding to her guests, she simply needed Cass to be there for her. Now Cass was going to be there, again, to witness the culmination of these three stressful weeks.

She was taking pains with her appearance today. Cass had nice legs that her mother lamented were "wasted" under her habitual trousers, and the bronze sheath she was wearing showed them to their best advantage, while the matching T-straps flattered her narrow feet.

Not one for half-measures, she lined her lids and applied mascara, then colored her mouth in a soft brown. Her amber jewelry picked up the color of her eyes and warmed her face, and she skipped the customary gel and allowed her hair to curl softly around her ears.

As she came downstairs, carrying a light coat and her purse, Dow let out a long wolf whistle. Cass smiled, knowing she had passed the femme test. Even Lesley was speechless for a moment.

"You look ... stunning," she finally said, admiration reflected in her eyes, and Cass indulged in a moment of vanity.

"You don't look bad yourself, Grandma," she laughed.

Lesley had resisted the matronly mother-of-the-groom look and was wearing a beaded jacket in dark blue, almost purple, over a matching silk tank and full, flowing pants. Her hair was confined in a French braid, and her only jewelry were small sapphire studs and her wedding bands.

"Well, ain't I the man?" Dow joked, extending his arms to both women. To his mother's dismay, but not her surprise, he had dumped his girlfriend shortly after hearing Seth's news. At his insistence, they sat in the back of the car and he chauffeured them to the reception. Generes was unable to make the wedding at such short notice, and each of them privately welcomed her absence.

Had Mrs. Bonnick been allowed three or four months to plan the reception, it could not have been more impressive. The house was decorated tastefully, the cake was magnificent and the food and champagne were excellent ¾ and plentiful. Soft jazz provided an unobtrusive complement.

Yoline was radiant in a loose dress of ivory lace, her hair upswept with a spray of baby's breath. It was difficult to tell she was expecting. Seth, resplendent in a soft grey suit he had been saving for graduation, had bought his bride a simple gold band with a delicate filigree pattern. They made an attractive, though slightly self-conscious, couple.

There were about forty guests dispersed throughout Mrs. Bonnick's pretty Cape. The older ones congregated in the living and dining rooms upstairs, while the younger crowd mostly stayed in the basement where the music was set up.

Cass met Yoline's family first. Despite the time pressure, several members of the clan had come from Panama, and there was a small collection of aunts, uncles and cousins in attendance. They were very cordial.

Lesley subsequently introduced Cass to her parents. Although they were completely gray, neither conveyed an impression of old age. They were still erect and their handshakes were strong. Cass knew from photographs that Lesley favored her mother, but she had her father's darker complexion, narrow eyes, and quiet personality. Sister Hillary was more assertive, aggressive even, holding Cass's hand for a while and scrutinizing her closely.

"I don't remember you," she said, in response to Lesley's introduction of Cass as her friend from high school.

"It was a long time ago," Cass covered smoothly. "We work together now."

She was glad to disengage her hand and move on to the next group comprised of Gene's brother and his wife (the resemblance was unmistakable), another couple whom Lesley introduced as Seth's godparents, and her friends Ginny and Leroy.

The speeches were short and heartfelt. Everybody liked the couple and genuinely wished them well. But it was Dow who was most affecting, as he spoke in his father's behalf, telling his brother that today he had become a man, the head of his own family, and that the future of the Gorton name had been entrusted, temporarily, to him.

He closed his speech with a quotation from Sophocles: "'One word frees us of all the weight and pain of life: That word is love.' I love you, Bro." The brothers hugged, grasping each other tightly and fighting back tears.

Mrs. Bonnick had prepared a feast that appealed to both Caribbean and American palates, and she practically glowed from the steady stream of compliments she received. Cass, sitting behind a heaped plate, felt like she was at Darlin's annual spread. She always used his sister's cooking as a point of comparison, and this was damn good.

Like the food, the selection of music was inclusive, and aside from the emotional moments when Lesley danced with Seth and Yoline trod the boards with her younger brother, the rest of the evening remained festive and light. Even Sister Hillary took to the floor with Dow when *The Electric Slide*, inevitably, was played.

Cass could not take her eyes off Lesley's mother as she slid and clapped in rhythms she had no doubt perfected in church. Catching sight of Mr. Hillary, Cass was not a little amazed to find that he, too, was mesmerized by his wife's turn on the floor. He had eyes for no one else as the crowd stepped up and back and shimmied from side to side, keeping time to the music.

It was a look that Cass recognized. "If only he knew," she mused, "that that is *exactly* the way his daughter makes me feel. When I look at her, everything else recedes and all my senses are filled with her."

The thought depressed her. Mr. Hillary could look at his wife with lyrical love or lustful longing, but she could display neither. What was so wrong with her feelings, anyway, Cass raged silently. Wasn't this a wedding, a celebration of love? Then why was it wrong to show her feelings here, of all places?

Suddenly, she wanted to stride across the room and tear Lesley away from Dr. Carter, one of Seth's professors, with whom she was engaged in conversation. She wanted to stop this damn charade. But the desire died at birth. She knew that, even if she dared, it would be a cheap gesture, benefiting no one, not even herself. So she smiled at Mr. Hillary, who had finally noticed her stare, and went in search of a drink. A stiff shot of Wray and Nephew should stand her straight. She smiled at her own wit.

Cass looked into the clear liquid and allowed self-pity to sit with her. So she was there for her woman. But what good was being there? What did she get for easing Seth over the hump, for jumping through hoops with his mother? Sure, he had hugged her and said thanks. Certainly, Lesley had been grateful and told her so. But where was her place? Exactly how did she fit in?   She felt hollow, like a vice president at an inaugural ball. Could she stand next to Lesley and bid the guests good night and thank them for coming? Of course not. And when they had all departed, could she put her arm around Lesley and walk her upstairs, sated and happy that everything had gone so well? Gene could. In fact, any *boyfriend* would be allowed to. Only she, Cass, could pay the piper yet never call the tune.

She was quiet on the drive back to Westbury, and Dow inquired if she was all right.

"Just a little fagged," she answered, deliberately, and feigned a yawn.

Later she lay wide awake in her designated bed and ached to be out of Gene's house and off his turf.

31

The Passat ate up the miles of I-95, as the soft spring air burbled through the little space between the window and the door frame. They had left early to avoid traffic, which was so light this Saturday morning they were able to hold hands while Lesley drove.

Tomorrow was Cass's birthday and a holiday mood was upon them. Lesley had packed a thermos of coffee, poppy-seed bagels already buttered, and fruit, and the radio kept them company. Occasionally, they would sing along, competing to see who knew all the words to the songs.

Cass was elated; she relished the idea of a weekend away from either of their families' eyes or influence. She genuinely loved Seth and enjoyed the get-togethers, but she had had enough of them all recently. Two weekends ago, she had trekked out to the Island, yet again, to celebrate Seth's graduation and send-off to Europe. Proud and handsome, the *cum laude* graduate had thanked her profusely for her support. His wife had thanked her also. One would think that Yoline's belly had just been waiting for the legitimacy of marriage, because she was abruptly, conspicuously pregnant compared to five weeks ago.

Anyway, here they were, whipping along the New England Thruway, gloriously alone. Lesley was amused by Cass's preoccupation with all things British; nevertheless, she had planned this getaway at a little English inn in Connecticut.

Lesley was quite familiar with the area, since she and Gene had been there on several antiquing trips. Every time they had gone there, they would promise to return for a weekend, but they never had. Lesley was glad now, although it seemed a little disloyal. But this was an experience Cass would enjoy and she wanted to be the one to give it to her.

It was just before 10:00 o'clock when they got to Mystic, and Cass fell in love immediately with the rustic charm of the little village, especially the quaint, old-fashioned street lights. When they got to the inn, she was completely won over. With a mere eight bedrooms, the old mansion was intimate and oh-so-English.

Cass inspected the antique furniture that graced the reception area while Lesley took care of business at the front desk. If the woman was surprised or curious, she certainly hid it well and was warm and friendly. She suggested they enjoy the late breakfast that was laid out in a charming little dining room that featured a fireplace. The two gourmands were delighted to comply, smiling at each other over huge waffles and fruit and sipping tea.

"We have to bring Mother here one day," Cass commented to Lesley, burping delicately as they finished. Her mother carried a lifelong nostalgia for her years in England.

They had taken the Painter's Room, which boasted a comfortable double bed covered by a lovely, crocheted bedspread, and old fashioned lamps. An unfinished painting, which partially captured the view from the window, stood on an easel, and on the dresser rested a palette of colors and some brushes in a vase. The theme was continued in the paint-splashed curtains.

There was also a television, which they were unlikely to use, and a chair with two tables occupied a little nook. The bathroom was small; there was only a shower stall, but while Cass crooned over the little embossed soaps, Lesley informed her that there was a Jacuzzi on the upper floor and she had reserved an hour later that evening.

"This is luvly, deah, so luvly," Cass drawled in a deep Cockney accent. "I wouldn't be a' tall surprised to see Her Majesty stop in."

Stuffed, sleepy and immoderately pleased, she was reluctant to leave the inn. But she fretted that it was a waste to come all this way simply to go to bed in the middle of the day.

"It's your treat," Lesley reminded her, "and you don't have to do anything but have a good time. We can take a nap now and go out later. And we've got all of tomorrow."

It was after 2:00 o'clock when they stirred, and even then there was no sense of urgency to get outdoors. They lay there, planning their trip to Antigua for Carnival in late July, discussing what they would buy Seth when he was ready to set up house, and generally enjoying the peace of being outside the City. It was slow, pleasant, comfortable conversation, and in this way, they passed another two hours.

Getting washed up and dressed ¾finally¾ they poked at each other good-naturedly, commenting on the weight they'd gained in the past nine months. "I like my little rolls, OK," Cass declared. "I was all bone until I got into my thirties, and I've earned these curves."

"I'd love to get rid of mine, but if it means I'll have to stop cooking and eat that packaged stuff, I guess I'll keep 'em."

"Fat and forty," Cass sang, "but, baby, baby, you're my meat." She grabbed Lesley by the waist and waltzed her around, both of them laughing with the relief that comes of having been weighed and found not wanting. Dressed at last, they looked at each other approvingly, high-fived, and sauntered out confidently.

Within walking distance of the inn were several antique shops with wares temptingly displayed outside. Lesley served as Cass's guide to both the neighborhood and the furniture that caught her eye. They weren't buying, just having fun browsing and trying to make up their minds about dinner.

Deciding on Italian, they strolled to a little place that Lesley knew well. The food was excellent, she said, and the service gracious. The two women felt deliciously romantic in the cozily lit eatery, the walls of which were decorated with scenes from the Old Country. Lesley was enjoying this, if possible, even more than Cass. Things were going well so far, and seeing Cass's eyes dance across the table completed her own pleasure. The way they laughed and talked lightheartedly reminded her of their first date, though she had not recognized it as such, at Tio Pepe's.

They began with warm, crusty bread, liberally coated with a delicious vegetable spread, and washed it down with a bracing red wine. Promising themselves that they would begin working-out right after this weekend, they enjoyed fried zucchini, followed by generous portions of calamari marinara over linguine. And since they would be exercising soon, they sampled a couple of the biggest canoli they had ever seen.

They *had* to walk ¾they were so full and tipsy¾ and they strolled around the area, admiring the architecture of the houses and wending their way back to the inn and their date with the jacuzzi.

If the inn was old London, then modern Connecticut certainly asserted itself upstairs, where the tub was located. Lesley and Cass luxuriated in the warm, pulsing water, eyes closed and lazy, satisfied smiles on their faces.

But the best part of the evening, as far as Cass was concerned, was when they returned to their room, their bodies warmly alive. For the first time since they had become intimate, Lesley took the initiative in their lovemaking. To say she was the aggressor would have been an exaggeration, but she took the lead, tentatively at first, then building up steam ¾literally¾ as she explored the body that already knew her own so well.

She was curious, then excited by what she was doing. To her surprise, she enjoyed exploring the textures, tastes and scents of the body that was so much like, yet different from, her own. She reveled in her power to make Cass arch, writhe and groan with pleasure. She marveled at her lover's unselfconsciousness, the way she lifted her body naturally and widened her thighs to facilitate the pleasure that Lesley was doling out.

Sated at last, they lay quietly entangled.

"How was I?" Lesley whispered anxiously.

"Baby," Cass smiled, eyes still closed, "you're the greatest."

******

"Happy birthday, hon!"

Cass sat up slowly. She had slept deeply and well in the unaccustomed silence. One never really experienced this degree of quiet in the City.

"Thanks, pet." She exaggerated a groan. "God, you wore me out last night, woman. Am I going to get the same kind of present this morning?" she asked, leering.

"If you're good."

"I'm good; I'm good."

"So you only want me for my body, huh?"

"Shoot! How'd you find out?"

Lesley shoved her playfully and, dramatically, Cass toppled over onto the floor.

They had a leisurely breakfast, but a healthy one, lingering over their cups of tea. The atmosphere of the inn did not inspire haste, but eventually they pushed back their chairs and left to explore the sights.

Parking on a side street, they crossed the drawbridge that led into the seaport. They whiled away a few hours browsing through the little shops, Lesley being careful to steer Cass away from the variety of chocolates and fudge that tempted the shopper. However, they lingered over the quilts, fingering their comforting beauty. Encouraged by Lesley, Cass selected a fan pattern in tan and green.

"Happy birthday," Lesley said again, as she plumped the package into Cass's arms.

"Thanks again," Cass said. "Another addition to the hope chest."

It became a little cool, but they agreed to have a late lunch at one of the outdoor cafes that punctuated the seaport. Somehow, the mood had changed with the weather, and the meal was very low-key. Lesley took her cue from Cass, who seemed engaged in some serious introspection. Probably thinking about getting older, Lesley mused.

"Lesley?"

"Mmm?"

"I want to thank you for this weekend, because you've made my birthday very special," Cass said, covering Lesley's hand with her own. She spoke crisply as though she had to get the words out before she broke down. "I'm a little sad right now, I'm sure you've noticed. Based on the way I feel about you and in this setting, in an ideal world, I would be asking you to marry me."

Lesley's eyes widened and her mouth fell open, but Cass wasn't finished.

"And one day, hopefully soon, I *will* get the opportunity to ask you. Because, trust me, society is going to wake up and realize that gays are people, too. With needs and desires. And they're not all physical."

She shifted, leaning over the table so she could look into Lesley's eyes.

"But until that time comes, pet, in my mind and in my heart, I'm going to think of you as my wife. Because you fill all my needs and my desires, and I want to spend the rest of my life with you."

Lesley could not respond; her throat was constricted by emotion. She had been married for twenty-four years, and she had never heard a speech as beautiful as this; in fact, she had never even received a marriage proposal. With Gene, there simply had been no time for this kind of romance. Time had been the enemy; necessity had carried the day.

She was grateful for the time she had now. And with the gift of time came choice. Nothing was being forced on her; there was nothing she *had* to do. She could stay or she could walk away. And she chose to stay.

The love they made when they returned to the inn went beyond the physical. There was mutuality of body and spirit. Each was giver; each was gift.

32

The fires cooled. They enjoyed their intimacies, but now Cass could look at Lesley without scorching her. Lesley could be apart from Cass without feeling alone. It was as though, knowing their spiritual reservoirs were full, their desperate thirst had been appeased.

Beyond dating now, they spent a great deal of time at home. The world and its pursuits receded, and the life they created within Cass's four walls was what mattered most.

Lesley tried to persuade Cass not to submit her article for publication. With only three years to go before she retired to the Caribbean, she reasoned, why make enemies now?

Cass discussed it with Sidra, a man of Haitian background with whom she had been friends since undergrad. They had been student teachers together, and they had supported each other's professional growth over the years. Neither made a career move without consulting the other. A dedicated principal and consummate politician, Sidra agreed with Lesley.

The article put aside, they were free to spend time with their books and music and watching TV. Cass appreciated television; it had been her companion during the two years before Lesley came into her life. They alternately cheered and cursed the Knicks as they made their championship bid; waged bets as to how the U.S. team would fare in the World Cup tournament; and, like the rest of America, watched and debated as O.J. Simpson was accused of murder.

But their favorite pastime was movies. For hours they would argue the merits of comedy, pitting Benny Hill against Monty Python, Robin Williams against Steve Martin. They mourned the fading of Richard

Pryor and the downfall of Woody Allen. And they nearly came to blows debating whether *Airplane* was funnier than *History of the World* or *Blazing Saddles.*

They'd been working their way for months through Cass's videotape collection and had determined their mutual favorites were *Fried Green Tomatoes, The Piano* and *The Color Purple.* A debate about some emotional point would invariably lead to another viewing to see who was right.

Lesley introduced Cass to her and Gene's favorites, *A Soldier's Story, Glory,* and, surprisingly, *The Little Mermaid.* Never particularly thrilled by war movies, Cass was moved to an appreciation of both the films and Gene.

In turn, she introduced Lesley to one of her personal favorites, *The Crying Game.* Cass confessed that, initially, she had seen it because she heard that Jody, one of the film's characters, hailed from Antigua. But the love story had seduced her, as it eventually did Lesley, leading Cass to share another favorite in the genre, *Kiss of the Spider Woman.* She also confessed that she found Raul Julia attractive ¾ to Lesley's amusement.

Despite the freedom that summer brought with its gloriously long days, they never found the time or inclination to walk or jog. Sure, they went to the park often. They even promised to buy the gear and learn to rollerblade like the hundreds of fanatics around them. But that, like every other outside thing, was unimportant. The women essentially loved their life together, just as it was, and felt no need to improve it, tone it, or tighten it.

Tomorrow, they were going to Westchester to celebrate July 4th at Marcus and Sylvie's. Lesley would make it up to the boys the following weekend with dinner. It would be the first time Cass would see Seth since he returned from his bike tour, and she was looking forward to hearing all about it and seeing Yoline's progress. They took bets as to whether Dow would bring the same girl he had brought to the graduation party.

As she had been careful to do in Antigua, Cass made sure that Lesley was introduced to everyone at her brother's barbecue. The easy acceptance caused Lesley to wonder if Cass regularly brought women to these gatherings, and curiosity, rather than jealousy, impelled her to ask.

"Please, Lesley. I don't bring casual dates around my family. You should know me better than that," Cass answered, a bit miffed.

Lesley was a bit chastened later that evening when, alone for a moment with Darlin', he told her how happy he was that Cass had someone this year. Usually, he said, the two of them ended up paired off. Not that they minded particularly, being such good friends and all, but he felt lonely being around the other couples and their kids year after year.

Come to think of it, he was right. There really were no singles at the party. But then, Lesley reasoned, most of Marcus and Sylvie's friends would be at the age when they'd be settled down and long married.

Lesley knew, because Cass had told her, that Marcus's wife had practically been hand-picked by his mother. Since he would not ¾or could not¾ choose, Roma did so for him, suggesting the young Bajan nurse whose quiet competence and self-possession so impressed her. They had been married within a year.

Lesley also knew, because she had experienced it firsthand, that among long-married couples, a single person was very much an outsider, if not an outright threat. And she recognized in Sylvie the type of woman who would neither invite nor tolerate a threat to her home life.

Matthew and his wife were at the barbecue, as they were every year. A big, handsome man, Matthew had a tough, shrewd look that no doubt made his job as a district attorney easier. His wife, Sharon, barely reached his shoulder; she was a plump, pretty woman who laughed easily. They had two sons, but they had not accompanied their parents.

There was no obvious tension between Cass and her oldest brother, but there was none of the easy familiarity she displayed with Marcus, or the unstudied affection she shared with Luke. Years before the blowup over the family house, she had come out to her brother during one of her then-frequent weekend visits.

"So Mother could have gone ahead and named you John, after all," had been his only response. Cass had been unable to determine whether it was amusement or sarcasm that colored his tone, but she knew it made a difference in the way he saw her. And sometimes, when he thought she was unaware of it, he would stare at her as if trying to see into her soul.

Later that evening, as they prepared for bed, Lesley commented on the fact that all of Cass's brothers had married either Antiguan or Caribbean women.

Cass shrugged. "For as long as my parents lived here, they never had any friends that were not West Indian. Other than school, we more or less kept to our own group, so West Indian women are pretty much who my brothers were exposed to socially."

"And you?"

"Quite frankly, I avoided them," Cass admitted. "New York can be a small place, and West Indians tend to know each other, or about each other. And I was always afraid someone would 'out' me to my parents before I got around to telling them."

She grinned. "And now I've given them their first American daughter-in-law."

33

They left early for Westbury since they needed to buy groceries. But it was much too hot to cook, and Cass persuaded Lesley to settle for salads and sandwiches and lots of iced tea.

By the time the kids turned up they were prepared. Seth and Yoline had picked up Dow and Elayne¾the same girlfriend¾at the station, and they arrived in a noisy heap, lugging beer and a huge watermelon.

The heat compelled them to eat in the relative shade of the backyard. Still, poor Yoline perspired profusely and fanned herself in vain. Seth eventually went indoors and returned triumphantly trailing an extension cord and dragging a fan.

"Don't say I don't know how to look after my wife," he declared, "and my son."

"Somebody's going to be disappointed," Yoline warned, "when the doctor says, 'It's a girl.'"

That led to a long and lively discussion of names, should the baby, indeed, be a girl. No matter how you arranged them, 'Lesley' and

'Myrlie' simply sounded terrible together, and there was no question of hurting either grandmother's feelings by choosing one name for their daughter. Elayne proposed a merger of Seth and Yoline, and everyone agreed on calling the baby Seline.

"But only if it's a girl," Cass reminded them, sending the group into gales of laughter.

Remembering that he had left photos from his trip in the car, Seth got up to fetch them. They passed the pictures around, remarking that, at last, it was cooling down.

Eventually, Lesley and Cass went into the house to carve the watermelon. Yoline also got up for yet another bathroom break, Seth playing the gallant husband and supporting her as she trundled across the yard.

"I like your family," Elayne said to Dow, watching Seth and Yoline. "They're cool. And your mother's old lady is a scream."

"My mother's old lady?" Dow repeated, eyes narrowing. "What do you mean my mother's old lady?"

"Come on, Dow," Elayne chided, "can't you see she's crazy about your mother? I noticed that the first time I met them, two months ago. Anybody can see that. "

"That's a load of bull!" he interrupted.

"O.K.," Elayne answered in amusement, throwing up her hands, "if you say so. But I think they make a cute couple."

Dow glared at her with immediate dislike. Yes, he thought, you West Coast perverted bitch, you'd think they were cute. He stalked off, leaving her sitting alone and unperturbed.

Dow was brilliant, Elayne mused, and his body was incredible, but she wasn't stupid enough to love him. She watched his behind appreciatively as he crossed the yard; even when furious, he was beautiful.

In the kitchen, Cass and Lesley were giggling like schoolgirls in church. Watermelon juice was spattered all over the front of their clothes and was seeping across the counter as they cut thick wedges from the fruit.

"Now, come on Miss Celie," Cass joked, as she fed Lesley a cube of the succulent pink flesh from the tip of the knife. "You know you done worked hard all day. Have a little bit o' this watermelon, won't you?"

"Don' mind if ah do, Shug; don' mind if ah do," Lesley drawled, opening wide.

"What the *fuck* is going on here?" Dow demanded ¾ although he knew. He had never seen or read *The Color Purple* and he had no idea who the characters were, but he knew intimacy when he saw it.

Lesley heard and saw Dow as though from a distance. She heard the ugliness of the words and saw the murderous anger in his face, even as she felt the cool sweetness on her tongue, the juice filling her mouth and slipping down her throat.

She watched Cass turn around, wordlessly, still holding the large knife. She knew that Dow wanted to lash out, to smash his fist into Cass. And she also knew, with certainty, that if he did, Cass would retaliate with the knife. All this passed through her mind at once, as though she were prescient, but she could neither speak nor act to prevent it.

Dow must have known it, too, because he made no move to act on his impulse. Instead, fists clenched, he raised his voice again, pain adding another dimension to his outrage.

"What the fuck is going on?" he screamed at his mother. "Is she screwing you?"

Not waiting for an answer, he turned on Cass.

"You damn bitch! In my father's house, too. ... Why don't you leave her alone? Find one of your own kind?"

He swung back to Lesley. "Is this why you kept running to the City? What's the matter with you? Daddy's not even cold in his grave yet and you've got this ... this ... bull-dagger in his place," he shouted accusingly.

Suddenly, Yoline burst into the kitchen, and Lesley marveled at the speed with which she was moving.

"Seth," the pregnant girl screamed. "Seth!" She didn't know what was going on. She had heard Dow bellowing profanely, and now Miss Shortman was standing there with a knife. "Oh, God! Seth!"

Seth came running, making a racket on the stairs, and crashed into Elayne, who had also rushed in from the backyard.

"Jesus Christ! What's wrong?" he shouted, looking with fright at the tableau.

"These two are gay, did you know that?" Dow spat out, his eyes never leaving his mother. "Yeah, they're sleeping together. With Daddy barely gone."

"Take it easy, man," Seth said, tugging at his brother and trying to lead him out. A vein in his forehead beat wildly.

"She's probably after your money, you fool," he said scathingly to Lesley, as he tried to shrug his brother off. "You think she doesn't know what she's doing? She knows the old man left you something. She's like some predator ¾ after the poor little widow.

"Are you that lonely, Mom?" he shouted again. "You couldn't wait for a man, a real man?"

"Dow! Chill, man, chill!" Seth was still struggling with his brother.

Cass wanted to smash him in the mouth and make him stop his ugly, hateful diatribe. But she was self-possessed enough to know that any move she made, anything she said, could wreck this family forever. Let Dow say what he liked, as long as he made no threatening moves on either of them. She turned to Lesley, who was staring at Dow with a bemused look on her face.

Elayne and Yoline were holding each other instinctively, frightened and wondering how a pleasant Saturday afternoon had turned into this.

"Just get your stuff and go, man," Seth pleaded, literally dragging Dow from the kitchen. "Just go. Leave them alone."

"Damn right, I'll leave them alone!" he declared. "And I'll never come back here. Never!"

Elayne ran after him, asking where he was going. She would never forgive herself for what she had started so casually. Seth begged Yoline to go after them, to take them to the station, and, again, she rushed off, her speed belying her girth.

"Mom, sit down," Seth urged, dragging a chair from the table. "Do you want some water? Miss Shortman, would you hand me some water?" He was frightened for his mother, who sat down obediently but refused the glass.

He turned to Cass. "What's wrong with her, Miss Shortman? Can't you make her say something?"

"Shock," Cass answered, surprised to hear her voice tremble. "It's just shock. Give her a few minutes."

34

Yoline and Cass cleaned up the kitchen and put things away, while Seth took care of the yard. They worked quietly and carefully, as if afraid to jar Lesley, who sat, monosyllabic, at the kitchen table.

At one point, Cass knelt before her, peering into her face, which was pinched and pained. Her skin felt too tight, somehow, and her chest hurt, as though someone had stomped all over it. She knew that Cass would stay, in fulfillment of the promise she had made that December night, but she wanted to be alone. So she roused herself to ask Seth to take Cass to the station when he left.

"I'll call when I get home," Cass promised, conflicted as to whether she should stay or go. Lesley could only nod to indicate she had heard.

She had no thoughts. She had a thousand thoughts. She thought she wanted to cry, but her eyes were dry, hot, staring. She tried squeezing her lids together to jump start the tears, but they wouldn't come.

This was not the way it was supposed to be; she shook her head. She had known the day would come when the kids must know about her and Cass, but she had assumed she would have gotten the chance to *tell* them. They weren't supposed to find out like this.

She'd done them a disservice; she really had. She'd done Cass a disservice, too. Cass had told her how excluded she had felt, ultimately, at Seth's wedding. And comparing the experience to her own initial feelings in Antigua, Lesley had empathized. But by taking her home, Cass also had taken the ultimate plunge and confirmed forever the speculation that she was gay. Lesley, on the other hand, had wanted to eat her cake and have it, too. Impossible, of course.

The phone rang and she grabbed it before it could ring again. It was Generes.

"Hi, Gen," Lesley forced some lightness into her voice. "What's up with you?"

"Not as much as with you, obviously," she replied coolly.

So Generes knew. Fine! Now they all knew.

"I just spoke to Dow," Generes continued. "What's going on, Lesley?"

"Well, if you just spoke to him, you already know what's going on, don't you?" She didn't want to be defensive; she didn't want another eruption on her hands, but she felt her hackles rise.

"I want to hear it from you. Is that woman your lover?"

That woman? Who was Generes calling *that woman?* For God's sake, she had been all over *that woman* at Christmas.

"Her name, as you well know, is Cassandra Shortman," Lesley answered slowly, carefully, "and, yes, she is my lover."

"What's the matter with you?" Generes shrieked. "You're not even embarrassed to say it?"

The scream grated on Lesley's shattered nerves and she held the phone away for a moment.

"What're you telling me, Lesley? That you're a lesbian?"

It was what Lesley had feared, dreaded, being asked. And now that the question was finally posed she still had not framed an answer.

"I'm not a lesbian, Generes," she denied, without vehemence.

"Then how is Cassandra Shortman your lover?" She spat the word lover as if it were phlegm on her tongue.

"Because she loves me. And I love her."

"Well, then, you *are* a lesbian," Generes stated flatly. "And, worse, a lesbian in denial."

"No, no," Lesley shook her head. "It's not like that. I don't want *women*. I'm not attracted to women that way. It's Cass. Just Cass."

"Lesley," Generes said patiently, as though her mother were a little slow, "women don't sleep with other women unless they're gay!"

"It's not about sleeping with her!" Lesley snapped, angry now. "We're friends, best friends. She cares about me. We do things together. We share everything. It's not just a physical relationship. You don't understand the difference she's made in my life. You just don't!"

Lesley attempted to explain. "Since your father's been gone, I've felt empty, alone. Like I was out of style, or something. Like I had no use. Cass changed all that."

"Everyone gets lonely at some time," Generes interrupted, "and that's why we have girl friends ¾ *platonic friends*."

"Like who? Eileen? Ginny? The last time I saw Ginny was at

Seth's wedding. She has her husband, her own life. What friends?"

"Lesley, there are groups for this sort of thing. Church outings and stuff, where you go to meet people. You're not a bad looking woman; you'd meet someone."

"But I met someone!" Lesley exploded.

"A man! Where you can meet a man!"

"Why does it have to be a man? Lots of women out there don't have a man. Lots of them have men they'd like to be rid of. You think everyone's like you¾gotta have a man?"

"At least I'm normal. I'm not the one sleeping with queers!"

"So, it's better to be promiscuous than gay; is that what you're saying?"

"Damn straight! Pardon the pun," she smirked sarcastically.

"You know, Generes, I'm surprised that you, of all people, would be so narrow and so mean," Lesley said with considerable bitterness. "When did I ever treat you that way? Every time you came home with some scheme, some plan, I supported you. I made excuses for you when you dropped out of college. When you were running around with boy after boy, I heard what the other kids were saying. I knew they were calling you 'Generous.' And you know what I did? I defended you! I went up against your father for you, time after time."

Generes was unfazed. "So what?" she asked sarcastically. "What am I supposed to do, trade off? Pretend that nothing's going on?"

"Why not?" her mother asked levelly. "You're good at it. When your student loan came due and you defaulted, nothing was going on. When you crashed your brother's car, it was just an accident, remember? You hadn't been drinking. No, nothing was going on. And when your father was dying ¾and dying to see you¾ you pretended that nothing was going on then. Why should anything be going on now?"

"Because it's affecting my brothers."

"I can't speak for Dow, but Seth is fine."

"Oh, yeah, I forgot that Cassandra Shortman's already bought him out. She got him a job in September, right?"

"Don't judge Seth by your standards, Generes. Not everyone sells out."

"But you don't mind selling Daddy out, huh?"

Lesley was livid. Had Generes been there, she would have floored her.

"What the hell do you know about Gene? When did you ever have the time to find out about him? Gene was a kind man, not vicious like you. You didn't know the first thing about him, other than when he got paid!"

But Generes knew she had found a sore spot and was willing to twist the knife.

"I hope you don't have that queer sleeping in Daddy's bed."

"Worry about who's sleeping in your bed for a change, Generes."

"Listen, Lesley ..."

"And don't call me Lesley, either," her mother cut her off. "I'm your mother, and if you can't remember that, then don't call me anything."

She hung up and sank to the floor, trembling.

Gene was right. He'd always been right. Generes was mean and selfish, a willful child who always had to have her own way. She had defended her too much and too long. She had never held Generes accountable for her actions, had spoiled her, had deferred to her and made the boys do the same.

Why? Because she had promised that when she had children she would treat them more warmly than her own mother had treated her and Lana. She had tried to foster a closeness with her daughter, who didn't want to be close to her. Generes responded only to Dowson Hillary, who had showered his first grandchild with attention and, unfortunately, money, as he had done with his own daughters. But Lesley and Lana had not exploited the man's weakness.

Generes was good at that. She knew her mother desperately wanted to be close to her, and she had made her pay for that closeness. She had begun by calling her mother by name, rejecting the authority that Lesley should have represented, and now she had dressed her down like a child. She had gotten Lesley down into the trenches with her, had muddied and bloodied her.

This was not the way a mother and daughter should act or react, Lesley reproached herself. Trading insult for insult. Hurling accusations and recriminations. Talking ugly; talking trash!

Seth, at least, had been decent. There had been no censure, no disgust; he had not even appeared shocked. He had made sure the doors and windows were secure before he gently said goodbye and urged his mother to get some sleep.

Could it be that he knew, had known all along? Was that why he had felt comfortable confiding in Cass, trusting her to break his news with gentleness and sensitivity? I'm always underestimating that boy, Lesley thought, sadly. I really don't know anything about him.

And Yoline. What does she think of this family now? She'll probably demand a divorce or something. Lesley laughed without enjoyment. Now I've managed to stigmatize poor Seth.

Dow has to be home by now, she thought suddenly. Should I call? No, *he* should call. He was rude and disrespectful and had no business talking to me like that. I'll wait for him to call and apologize.

But suppose he never does? The thought made her whimper unconsciously.

35

Seth offered to drive Cass right into the City, but she declined. She, too, needed time alone to think, to recover her composure. Shaken by the confrontation, she was, in fact, relieved that Lesley had sent her home.

Dow's viciousness had shocked her. She knew homophobia, of course; she had spent her life trying to avoid becoming another one of its casualties. But it had been a long time since she had encountered it in such a virulent form. Granted, Dow had been shocked, perhaps even scared, by what he had discovered. But to be so mean! What had she done to deserve that; what had Lesley done?

Why did some people think that gays didn't have feelings, didn't have souls? Did they assume that gays were born with some sort of thick skin that simply deflected insults? Cass ¾and every gay friend she had¾ kept an unwritten catalog of every rejection, snub or slight that was thrown her way. Sometimes she retaliated immediately; at other times, she slowly punished that person for life. Dow would fall in the latter category, even if he mended fences with his mother.

Cass couldn't help but be afraid of how the day's events would affect Lesley; how it would affect their relationship. Sure, she had agreed to be with her, even to move with her eventually to Antigua. But that was before the fabric of her family had split at the seams. Would Lesley now feel compelled to mend it at any cost?

If Lesley were like Roma, then Cass was in trouble, because Mrs. Shortman would walk barefoot through hell for her children. But then again, the situation would never have gotten to this, because Roma had never conceded authority to her kids. They had always known, even Matthew, who was in charge. That was the trouble, Cass felt; Lesley had raised her children to regard themselves as her peers.

Though she knew there was nothing to be gained from assigning blame, Cass still fretted. Why didn't I insist she tell her kids; why? I knew no good could come of keeping it from them. I told her I was willing to be there, to stand up with her while she told them. I promised her I would. Why did she keep it from them? Why did she do this to us?

She was home for more than an hour before she was rational enough to call Westbury.

"Yes?" Lesley was almost hostile as she answered the phone.

"It's me. What's the matter?"

"Sorry. I just hung up from Generes and I thought she was calling back."

"What'd she say?"

"Dow called her."

"And?"

"Not good."

"She didn't understand, huh?"

"To put it mildly, no, she didn't." She sighed heavily. "It was awful, Cass, awful. She was mean and nasty, and I'm embarrassed to admit that I was, too."

"Well, I'm sure you were justified," Cass defended Lesley.

"Maybe. But she made me feel cheap."

"Cheap?" Cass's voice went up a register. "What'd she call you?"

"No, not like that. I mean our relationship, as mother and daughter, feels cheapened, somehow. She called me a lesbian, of course, but it's not even that. I feel I don't know her. Well, no, that's not true. It's more like I'm knowing her for the first time. Not the way I've been seeing her. The way she really is. And I don't like her, Cass. I don't."

"I see," was all Cass replied to that. She didn't particularly want to hear what Generes had said. She had reached her own conclusions and didn't want to have to add Lesley's daughter to her 'bad book.'

"So how are you feeling now, pet?" she asked solicitously. "Will you be all right?"

"I don't know if I'll *ever* be all right. She said I was selling out Gene," Lesley burst out.

"She said that just to hurt you," Cass told her. "From everything I've heard about him, Gene wasn't the judgmental type. You don't need to be listening to Generes, anyway. He was your husband; you know him better. ... Did Dow call back?"

"No."

Cass sighed. "Are you going to bed, then, or do you want to come in?"

"No."

"Well, what do you want to do?"

"I don't know," Lesley responded dully. "I just don't know."

"Oh, pet, don't brood about it. Just give him a little time. He's upset right now, you know. Generes is upset, too. It's a shock to them."

"Seth surprised me. Did you ever say anything to him, Cass?"

"Never! I was surprised, myself. Even on the way to the train, he kept talking about the baby and how he hoped it would be a boy ¾ as if nothing had happened. It's obvious he knew, but no, I never told him." She couldn't resist a dig: "It wasn't in my place to tell him."

But Lesley was too distracted to notice. "Do you think I should call Dow tomorrow?" she asked tentatively.

"Do you want to, Lesley?" Cass could feel her ire begin to rise again. Was the woman going to go crawling to him, for God's sake?

"Not really. First, I can't believe he called Generes to complain about me. He never calls her, never! She doesn't call him either. Now they're in cahoots against me!

"I never expected them to congratulate me, Cass. I wasn't expecting a gold medal. But what do they want to do ¾ live their lives *and* mine?"

133

Cass murmured sympathetically. This was the attitude she would rather Lesley adopt. She wanted to see the angry woman who, a couple months ago, had threatened to choke her sons if they didn't stop fighting. It was time¾high time¾she defended herself for a change.

"I'm only 43 years old. What does Dow want me to do? Sit around and wait to collect Social Security? Putter around the house waiting until he makes his once-a-month visit for a real meal and to play his piano?" Her voice cracked. "Does he ever think about me? I don't mean as his mother. As a *person!* I'm not going to sit around and mourn Gene the rest of my life, Cass; I'm not!"

Cass wanted to remind her they were on the same side, but she realized that Lesley's anger was yielding to tears, and so she said nothing.

"I gave Gene and those kids twenty-four years of my life. Twenty-four! I was a good mother, Cass. And a good wife. I always put them first. Do you know how long it took me to get through undergrad? Six years! I read my kids to sleep, you hear? I read them Winnie the Pooh, so they'd grow up normal. And I read them African folk tales, so they'd be proud of their heritage. I tried to do it right. And I cooked for them from scratch. I never opened a can for them in my life.

"Generes? I took her to ballet, then she wanted to take tap, then tennis, then skating. And Girl Scouts. And Dow? You don't know how many years I had to listen to him banging on that piano. I'd try to study ... I'd have to leave ... go to the library. I'd come back and he'd still be banging, banging, banging." She was disjointed and hiccuping now. "I typed his papers before I did mine. I did his research! I don't even know how I got through school and raised a family. I don't. When does my turn come, Cass? When is it *my* turn?"

"It *is* your turn, pet," Cass soothed. "Sometimes you just have to take it, you know. You can't wait until someone gives it to you. But it's your turn. It's our turn. And it'll be OK, I promise."

36

She had gotten used to Lesley's companionship, her presence at the little kitchen table, her body in the bed. Now Cass felt achingly alone, bereft, like there had been a death in the family. In fact, the last time she felt like this had been when her grandmother died. But Lesley wasn't dead; she was merely brooding. For a whole week she had been holed up in Westbury, protesting that she wouldn't be good company, and inevitably, an emotionally strained Cass had exploded at her over the phone.

"So why the hell you don't call him then?" she shouted at Lesley, Antiguan accent uppermost.

"Call who?"

"Dow! You know that's why you're staying out there. Why you don't just call him and get it over with? You driving me crazy already with this shit!"

Lesley got her back up. "Look, Cass, don't push me, OK."

"Push you? Push you? When did *I* ever push you? I'm not the one pushing you, Lesley Gorton. Don't confuse me with your son. He's the one pushing you ¾ right over the fuckin' edge!"

The silence pulsed with anger and regret.

"Look," Lesley finally said, "it's obvious you feel that I'm stringing you along, and I really am sorry about that. But right now, Cass, I don't feel like coming into Manhattan! My family is screwed up, and I'm the one who did it, and I feel rotten. When I feel better ¾and I'm trying to¾ you'll be the first to know. Fine?"

"Fine!"

God alone knew whether the relationship would withstand this crisis.

Cass had promised Lesley that she would be there for her, but Lesley was shutting her out. She felt she had done the wrong thing. What was the use of anger now? Hadn't enough harm been done? Soft words and persuasive arguments might have opened the door, but she had probably closed it more securely by hurling recriminations and screaming profanity. What was the point of making the relationship adversarial?

It had been three silent days since the fight, and Cass just knew that she would be traveling alone to Antigua. She didn't know if she should go on her own or cancel the trip. But what good was hanging around Manhattan feeling miserable when she could be enjoying the company and comfort of her friends and relatives? Lesley wasn't the only one with a family!

Lesley called, finally, early that evening and got straight to the point. "Cass, I'm not going to Antigua after all. I'm sorry to disappoint you and your family, but this isn't a good time for me." She sounded like she was reading from a prepared speech.

"Maybe if you came, you'd feel better," Cass offered in a conciliatory tone. "There's a lot going on at Carnival, and it'll take your mind off things."

"No, but thanks, anyway. I'm dealing with some problems right now, and I have to resolve them first."

"Like what?"

"Stuff. I can't get into it right now, Cass. Just trust me, OK."

Cass inquired about Seth and Yoline, and they made small talk for a while. Lesley promised to see Cass before she left for Antigua.

Quite frankly, Cass didn't believe her. Depressed and afraid, she took off for Astoria, not even bothering to call ahead. It was still light out, she reasoned, and if Darlin wasn't home, she'd wait around. In fact, she waited for more than an hour, but Darlin never showed up, and Cass returned home feeling lower than when she left. It seemed as though all the people she counted on were unavailable when she needed them most, and she struggled not to give in to self-pity.

The night before Cass left on vacation, Lesley left a message on the machine saying she couldn't come to the City after all.

"Tell your parents I'm sorry I can't make it," she said, "and give Celeste and Dell my love. And Luke and the kids, too, of course. Take lots of pictures. Have a safe trip, Cass, and have a good time for both of us. I love you."

To Cass's ears, it sounded like goodbye.

The American Airlines terminal was packed with Antiguans going home for the festival, and while she was checking in, Cass chatted bravely with people she knew. She and Lesley had purchased first-class tickets once again, and on board she was relieved not to recognize anyone sitting up front.

She could not help remembering the last time she had done this. How happy and excited she had been. Not even the realization that her father might, at last, question her sexual orientation had been enough to dampen her feelings then.

They had been looking forward to this second trip so much, had even begun fantasizing about the life they would have when they retired to the island.

Now, all their plans might remain just that, a fantasy. Cass cried, her face turned to the little window where the clouds were covering the sun.

37

I'm being a coward, an emotional invalid, Lesley admitted, as she lay watching the progress of the sun through the stained-glass window. Why can't I just ask Seth? He calls every morning at 7:00 and every evening just after the 11:00 o'clock news, asking me if I'm all right, do I need anything, should he come out. And every day I reassure him that I'm fine, that I need nothing, and that he shouldn't bother driving out here. What can I lose by asking him?

The phone rang on the hour and they went through the routine. Lesley inquired about Yoline, who had a doctor's appointment later that day, and they discussed his hunt for an affordable two-bedroom apartment.

"Seth?" Lesley steeled herself. "You knew all along, didn't you, about me and Cass?"

"Yeah, I guess."

"How? Was it something we did? Something I said?" The questions tumbled out now. "How come you didn't react like your brother?"

"Whoa, Mom. One at a time," Seth said. In fact, he was stalling. He didn't know where to begin or how to answer.

"OK, OK," Lesley agreed. "When did you find out?"

"In December. On Christmas Day, actually, when Generes stayed out so long with the car."

"What?" Lesley was puzzled. "What's Generes got to do with this?"

"Well, as soon as I met Miss Shortman, I figured she was gay," Seth explained, "and Yoline did, too, when she met her. But I just thought she was a friend of yours from high school, like you said. We thought you were seeing someone ¾a man¾ in the City, and Miss Shortman was just covering for you. And that was fine. I was happy for you ... relieved, you know."

Seth was unable to confess exactly how relieved he had been to think his mother was dating. How much lighter he had felt about not having to look after her. True, she'd never complained; she'd never asked him to move back home to be with her. Yet, he had felt a burden of responsibility the others didn't feel, couldn't feel, since they'd moved out before their father had become ill. And with the relief of her being with someone, rather than at home brooding, had come guilt. She was his mother after all, he had scolded himself, and a good mother, at that. He should have been happy to look out for her; instead, he was happy he no longer had to.

He shook himself mentally and continued.

"Then, remember when Dow was playing the piano and we were singing?"

"Uh huh," Lesley encouraged.

"Well, I felt she was telling you something, Mom. I don't remember the song, exactly, but I remember wondering if there was a message she was trying to get across. And then later, I knew. We were sitting in the kitchen and you were scared about Generes, why she was gone so long with the car, and Miss Shortman just kept talking, so there wouldn't be any silences, you know. And I knew she wasn't just talking because she was interested in me. I could tell that she was doing it for *you*. I could see it in her face when she looked at you. And I just knew... ." He trailed off.

"I see," Lesley said quietly, marvelling at his perception and wondering again how she had managed to underestimate her son so badly. "How come you didn't get mad? Why didn't you say something?"

"Say *what*, Mom?" he asked. "I saw the way she looked at you. I saw how happy you were. What was I going to say? 'Stop it!'

"I wasn't disgusted, if that's what you're asking," he said. "Me and Yoline have friends who're gay, men and women, and we hang out with them all the time. Of course, it's a bit different when it's your own mother," he conceded with an embarrassed laugh. "You don't even want to believe your own parents are having sex, for God's sake, so you just don't think about it. But, as Yoline said, if I love you, how can I be upset that Miss Shortman loves you?"

"Thanks, Seth. That's very generous of you." Lesley drew a deep breath to steady herself. "Cass wanted us to discuss the relationship, but it was difficult, you see, because you kids meant so much to me, especially with your dad being gone. I didn't want you to hate me, or look at me with disgust, because I was with a woman. And now look at what's happened anyway... ." She began to cry quietly.

"Nobody hates you, Mom," Seth said gently. "Generes and Dow will come around. They just need time, that's all. They don't hate you."

"I couldn't leave Cass, because she meant so much to me," Lesley sobbed. "I was trying to keep both sides of my life going, because I wanted all of you in it. I love you and Dow and Generes, but you're all moving on. Cass was mine; she was there for keeps. I was so happy, Seth. And now I feel like God is punishing me."

"Stop it! You're talking like Gramma," Seth reprimanded her. "You think God would be so mean?"

38

Ordinarily, Cass had a full schedule for the Carnival season, sometimes staying in town for days at a time. Her parents didn't complain; it was enough to know their daughter was on the island. Their turn would come, anyway, after the celebrations ended and she dragged herself, tired and hoarse, back to the country.

This trip, Cass couldn't rouse herself to go into St. John's. To everyone who called, Mrs. Shortman reported that her daughter was under the weather. Cass was heartsick, and she complained of feeling logy.

Her father proffered his timeless remedy. "Girl, a good sea-bath is what you need," he declared. And despite her objections, Cass found herself accompanying him to Half Moon Bay three mornings in a row. But not even the glory of a Caribbean sunrise could lighten her gloom.

Celeste, on the other hand, decided that Cass had not been eating properly and offered scathing remarks about American fast food. And Cass didn't have the energy to disabuse her, so she dutifully ate the steamed fish, mangoes and papaya and whatever Celeste put on the table.

She was animated only when Luke and Dell brought the kids over, gratified to see that Lucas not only remembered her, but competed with his sister for their aunt's attention.

Roma watched her daughter and worried. Concern made her corner Cass in the bathroom one morning.

"C'sandra, what really happened that Lesley didn't come with you? You-all mash up or something?"

Cass shrugged. "To tell you the truth, Mother, I don't know."

"What you mean you don't know? She found somebody else?"

"No. But her kids found out."

"You mean they didn't know?" She was incredulous. "What's really going on here? You said you were going to talk to me in February, and you left without telling me a thing. I don't understand this set-up."

Sitting on the side of the tub, Cass stared at her mother, who was unconsciously barring the door, arms crossed and expectant. She sighed.

"I told you she's a widow and she has three kids, right? Well, the older two found out about us ¾one told the other¾ and they went *off!* There was a big scene at the house with Dow, and he cussed us and walked out. Then the daughter called, and she and Lesley had it out on the phone. Now nobody's talking to anybody. Including me, it seems."

"What about the other boy?"

"Seth. He's not a boy anymore. He just got married and his wife is expecting a baby in September. *He* took it well; I think he knew all along. Don't ask me how," she said, forestalling her mother, "because I don't know.

"Anyway, the upshot is that I haven't seen Lesley since," she continued bitterly. "We've only spoken on the phone. *I* know she's staying in New York hoping they'll call her, although she won't admit it. *She* says she has things to figure out. Yeah, and I was born yesterday!"

Roma digested her daughter's outburst.

"C'sandra," she said, thoughtfully, "you know why we moved to the States?"

"Because you wanted us to go to college," Cass answered dully.

"You went to college because you were there already," her mother corrected. "And you have to take advantage of your opportunities, after all.... . No, we moved because of your father."

"Daddy?"

"Your father had a woman from Freetown," Roma recounted, her eyes narrowing with the memory. "I talked to him about it, and your grandmother warned him, too, but he wouldn't stop from her. So, I told him flat: 'Listen: I came down here to nurse my mother, and when she died I was prepared to go back to London. *You asked me to stay here and marry you. Now, after all these years, you expect me to put up with you and your keep-woman and subject my children to that slackness? Well, I have news for you!*'

"Then I called your Uncle Llewellyn in Queens, and I made plans to leave. And guess what? By the time everything was organized, Drury told me he was coming, too; he wasn't about to sacrifice his family for some outside woman. But I already figured that out; I had packed his suitcase and he didn't even know!" Roma actually laughed, remembering her victory.

"Why you telling me this now?" Cass asked, annoyed. "You should know it's not going to change the way I feel about Daddy."

"Is OK. It didn't change the way I feel about him."

"Who's the woman? I know her?"

"No, she died long-long time."

Cass was relieved. Had the woman been alive, she would have hated her passionately for threatening her mother's security. Conversely, all she felt about her father was relief that he had chosen his family.

But with relief came another perspective, and she understood then why her mother had told the story. She was forcing her to see Dow and Generes in a different light, and, by extension, Lesley's position. Suddenly, Cass saw herself as the "outside woman" who threatened Lesley's family, and she was ashamed of her anger and impatience.

Would Lesley be as determined to protect her children as Roma had been? Cass trembled at the possibility.

"And that was supposed to make me feel *better?*" she asked her mother plaintively.

"I told you the story so you could prepare for the worst," Roma answered, "and hope for the best."

"Hope? I didn't hear any reason to hope."

"Only the dead don't have hope, C'sandra," was her mother's sage reply.

39

There was a letter from Generes sitting on the kitchen table. It had come yesterday but Lesley could not bring herself to open it. Despite Seth's reassurances, she was afraid of the condemnation the letter might contain, but more than that, she was tired. Tired of the oppressive loneliness, the pointless isolation, the simple boredom of waiting for things to happen. Waiting for Dow to call. Waiting for things to fall into place. Waiting to get the nerve to do one thing or another. She felt as though her life was on hold and the other party was really never coming back on the line; at the same time, she was afraid to hang up.

She needed to be occupied. Grabbing a can of Old English and a dust cloth, she began polishing the furniture with brisk, concentrated movements. Staring at the pictures above, she glossed the piano, thinking that she missed Dow and the music he had made, the life he had brought to this room on the Sundays he visited. Abstractedly, she ran her fingers over the keys, picking out a chord here and there. Before she realized it, she was sitting down at the instrument and playing as though she had never stopped. *Moon River.* Cass loved this particular piece and played the CD almost every Sunday; she said it reminded her of her father.

Funny, Lesley mused, I'm missing Dow, but I'm playing Cass's music. She played easily, effortlessly, as she ruminated. Mama said I was no good; said I had no ear. But listen to me now: I don't need Mama's approval and I don't need Dow to play, either. I can make my own music.

Her fingers moved surely and gracefully over the keys and she felt a peace descend upon her. When Cass comes back, she thought, I'll play for her.

She stopped abruptly. How do I know for sure that Cass is coming back to me? Fear punched her. Oh, God! Why *should* she come back to me? I've been treating her exactly the way my kids have been treating me. I'm gambling on her, taking her for granted, and just assuming

143

she'll be there when I've worked things out. And I think *Generes* is selfish?

There was a brief cacophony as Lesley pushed herself away and ran for the phone. Two thousand miles away Mrs. Shortman answered and said, regretfully, that Cass had gone out with her brother. Lesley's shoulders slumped; I could've been there, she told herself with regret. She forced herself to make pleasant conversation with Roma, charging her to make sure Cass knew she had called.

Holding the phone to her chest, Lesley chided herself for being crushed. "It's Carnival," she said to herself sternly. "Didn't you think she'd go out and have a good time? She *should* forget you! You've ignored her for weeks."

Impulsively, she dialed again. Maybe she's at Luke's house; she crossed her fingers.

Dell answered. She recognized Lesley's voice immediately.

"You at the airport?" she asked, laughing. "I'll pick you up in ten minutes."

"I wish! How're you? How's Luke and the kids?"

"Fine, everybody's fine. They went into town with C'sandra and they're not back yet."

"I was hoping to talk to Cass," Lesley said, her disappointment stark. "Her mother said she was with Luke, so... ."

"Well, I'll tell her to call you."

"No, that's OK. I really wanted to surprise her. I'll call again. When's a good time?"

"Tomorrow we're going to a picnic and, later on, to the calypso show. After that she won't go home until Wednesday, probably. This is the big weekend, you know. You'd have to catch her tomorrow morning right after church."

Dell paused. "I thought the two of you broke up."

"She said that?" Lesley's stomach lurched upward into her chest and constricted her heart.

"She hasn't said *anything*. She just stays home all the time. Not even Luke knows for sure what's wrong. She just said she's not feeling too good. You-all had an argument?"

"It's my fault!" Lesley burst out. "The kids found out about us, and it was awful, just awful."

"They couldn't 'find out' if you didn't hide it," Dell commented dryly.

Lesley winced. She had witnessed Dell's directness in February, but then it had been directed at Luke and Cass.

"How come you didn't tell them?" Dell persisted.

"Scared, I guess. Scared they'd be mad and stop speaking to me."

"And so you stopped speaking to C'sandra because your kids not speaking to you?"

"I never stopped speaking to her!" Lesley said defensively. "I just needed some time to think."

"But, Lesley," Dell pointed out with patience, "you must have been thinking about the possibility all along. What's there to think about now?"

"I was wondering how to reach my kids. Patch things up, I mean."

"Suppose they tell you to give up C'sandra? You going to do it?"

"That's what I'm afraid they'll say. And I don't want to do it, Dell; I really don't. I got a letter from my daughter, and I can't even open it."

"Your children are big people, Lesley; you have to live your own life," Dell chided. "My mother lived her whole life for me, and by the time she should have been living for herself ¾ bam! She was gone. Work and worry killed her. See me? I'm so glad my kids are big enough for me to leave them. I pack them off to their grandparents every so often, and me and Luke go away for a weekend. Puerto Rico, St. Thomas, Montserrat. We fly for free, and I make sure we take advantage of it! Luke's first wife always put her children in front of him, and you see what happened... ."

"Yeah, I guess you're right," Lesley said, doubtfully.

"Who's there with you?"

"No one's here. It's just me."

"Ah! Who's with your kids?"

"Who knows?" Lesley laughed. "Every time I talk to my daughter, she has a new boyfriend. And Dow changes girlfriends like other people change socks. The youngest one just got married, you know; his wife is expecting."

"OK, then. All of them have their own lives. None of them going to move back in with you. You need to talk to them, girl. Tell them you love them, but this is your life."

145

"It's the gay thing that's bothering them, though," Lesley said, with quiet anguish. "They're not going to accept me being with a woman."

"And what makes you so sure they would accept a man any better? And if they did, how do *you* know this man would treat you as well as Cassandra?"

"Yeah, you're right." She laughed, but shakily. "You're right. Tell you what: I'll talk to them and if they don't come around, I'll give you their numbers and you can call them, OK?"

"You do that," Dell agreed, darkly.

Lesley thought after she hung up. Really, how do I know they'd accept any man after their father? She'd worked on cases like that. Granted, those were younger children, but how old did one have to be to get past those feelings? Hadn't her own mother practically rejected her daughters after her only boy was killed?

Thinking about it exhausted Lesley, and she threw herself across the daybed on the enclosed porch. Although it was early, she slept deeply and long; she dreamed that Dell was spanking Dow.

She awoke with the dream fresh in her mind and went to the phone. Not that she expected him to be home ¾on Saturday nights he went to the Village to hear jazz ¾but she didn't want to get cold feet waiting until tomorrow.

The machine came on and she was brief: "Dow, it's Mom. I'm sorry about what happened, and I'd like us to talk about it. Call me tomorrow. Please, son." She felt better, lighter.

She crawled back into bed, with a box of macaroons and a carton of milk
to counteract the inevitable heartburn, and read Generes's letter:

Dear Lesley:

OK, so the last thing you told me was not to call you Lesley, but how do you   expect me to stop after almost 26 years? You're my mother; will calling you Mom make me any more or less your daughter? We're adults anyway, aren't we?

I've been thinking about some of the things you said that night, and I'm sorry that it seemed I wasn't there for Dad when he was dying. It was a big deal for me, believe it or not, but I couldn't cope with being there. He was too young to die, you see, and I'm not good at death.

One of the things that comforts me about being a flight attendant is that if anything goes wrong, it'll be quick, no long suffering.

I spoke to Seth several times and I promised him I'd call, but I can't do that either. (Seems like there's a lot of things I can't deal with, right?) Anyway, I never knew you were so lonely, Lesley. You always sounded upbeat, so I really thought you had gotten over Dad's death by now. I didn't think it would drive you to this. Maybe you should have sold the house and gotten away from the memories, you know. Made a fresh start.

Maybe you and I can make a fresh start ourselves. I'm sorry about the things I said that night, and I know you're sorry about the things you said, too. I'm prepared to forgive so we can go back to having fun like we used to. Who knows, maybe you can even come to Miami for Labor Day and visit with me.

In the meantime, I'll keep my fingers crossed that you meet someone nice. At least the baby will be here soon and you'll have your hands full then. I know how grandparents are.

Love, Generes.

Relief made Lesley weak. It made her laugh. For this her stomach had churned? Generes was only being her old self, burying her head and pretending that things were the way she saw them. She wanted to pity her daughter for her naïveté, but then hadn't she, Lesley, been the same? Hadn't she hoped that she could avoid this situation by ignoring it?

It would serve no useful purpose to antagonize Generes, but it would take a lot of diplomacy to explain to her daughter that this was not about missing Gene. To remind her that she had already met someone nice. To tell her she had nothing to apologize for and that she would not end her relationship so they could go back to having fun. And to inform her that she was a young, vibrant woman who was not about to settle for being only a grandmother.

Lesley sat at the kitchen table with a fresh writing tablet. Her daughter was right. They were two adults; they would simply have to find some other middle ground on which to meet. It was three in the morning when she finished opening her heart to Generes.

Not surprisingly, she overslept the next day. When she called the Shortman household, there was no answer.

40

The Shortmans leaned against the fence that surrounded Government House, the overhanging trees providing a welcome shade. Ordinarily, Mr. Shortman could not be bothered to watch the parade, preferring to spend his time drinking with his cronies and discussing local politics. But the family had turned out to see Amaya and Lucas, who were in the parade for the first time, and Luke was poised with his camcorder.

The sun blazed and the parade route was long. Armed with juice boxes, sunscreen and an umbrella, Dell had decided to walk alongside her children's troupe to make sure they didn't blister or become dehydrated. She would carry Lucas, if necessary.

Maintaining conversation with her family and the crowd, in general; swaying to the infectious sounds of the steelbands passing atop trucks; and snapping photographs of the often-stunning costumes and lively children, Cass remained disquieted. She had been unable to put Lesley's call out of her mind. Her mother had reported that Lesley sounded pleasant and upbeat, though disappointed at not finding Cass at home.

Cass was alternately relieved to know that Lesley had been in touch and upset that she had called. Who was Lesley, she asked herself one minute, to think she could "fling and catch" her like that? Who? The next minute she was dying to hear her voice. But fear and the desire to hang tough prevented her from returning the call. She would be back in New York soon enough to have her heart broken.

Starting that night, she threw herself into the national spirit of music, raunch and sweat. Carnival, after all, was for forgetting, not merely the differences of creed and class, but the everyday cares and concerns that beset the living. And because the climax of the the festival was so concentrated, whenever Cass managed to sleep, over the next few days, it was the sleep of the exhausted, leaving her no time for thought, no memory for dreams.

As Dell had predicted, Cass did not return to her parents' house until the festivities ended. On Wednesday night she welcomed the peace of the countryside, lying in the hammock on the porch and talking with her mother.

They heard the phone ring and Drury answer. His hearty laugh punctuated the conversation and the quiet night. After a few minutes he called Cass inside and, handing her the receiver, squeezed her shoulder before leaving the room.

She expected to hear her godfather's voice, or Luke's.

"Hello?"

"Hi, Cass."

Her body suddenly felt warm and her knees liquid at the sound of Lesley's soft, confidential voice. Perspiration appeared on her forehead.

"Cass?" Concern tinged Lesley's voice.

"Hi," was all she could manage.

"Your dad's still there?"

"Uh-uh."

"How are you doing? You miss me?"

"Fine," she answered, recovering. "Yeah, I guess.... How are you?"

"I'm good. Good. Better than when you left."

"How's Seth and Yoline? Wait! Did the baby come?"

Lesley laughed lightly. "No, Cass. That's not why I called; I just wanted to touch base, see how you were, that's all. I miss you."

"Well, it's nice to know you remember me," she replied, a little accusatory.

"I'm always thinking about you, Cass," Lesley reassured. "I called on Saturday because I had a surprise for you."

"A surprise? What?"

"A song. I was playing a song, *Moon River*, actually, and I wanted you to hear it."

This was not going easily; Cass was giving no ground. Lesley actually felt silly; silly and embarrassed, as though she was giving a gift that was unwanted but acknowledged out of mere politeness.

"That's great." Cass forced enthusiasm into her voice. "How come you're playing again?"

"I was thinking about you, and before I knew it, I just started. I surprised myself, believe me."

"I'm happy for you." She took a deep breath. "Who're you playing with?"

Lesley decided not to play games. "No, I haven't heard from Dow. I called and left a message, but I haven't heard from him."

"So nothing's resolved, then?"

"I'm not thinking about it."

"I see."

How had the conversation gone downhill so fast, Lesley wondered. Where was the welcome back? The relief? Why was there nothing to say?

"Are you still coming home on Saturday?" she asked.

"Up till now," Cass replied guardedly.

"Want me to come pick you up?"

"No, I'm not sure when I'll get in. I'm taking the morning flight out of here, and I'm going to try to connect ahead of schedule in Puerto Rico. But I don't know if I'll manage to do that, so I wouldn't want you to wait. I'll be home by four or so, the latest. Back in the City, I mean."

"OK," Lesley said softly, "I'll meet you there later. I promise. We have a lot to talk about. Tell your mom goodnight for me. And enjoy the rest of the trip. Love you."

Sure, you do, Cass thought, cynically, listening to the dial tone. You love me now, but will you love me when Dow gets through with you?

She felt a headache coming on. Now, what had her father meant by that gesture?

******

Lesley felt Cass's wariness and knew she was steeling herself against anticipated pain. Based on the past month, she couldn't blame her. A month already? My, word! By the time Cass got back, it would be a month since the incident. No wonder she sounded so disassociated.

She understood. That was how she was beginning to feel about her son. Dow had not responded to her message. He was in town, she knew, because Seth had said nothing to the contrary. But she was becoming inured and her anxiety over their relationship was receding. What was it that her friend Gael used to say: Too long a wait can make a stone of the heart. She and Cass were getting tired of their respective waits.

Actually, she needed to call Gael, who was the family's lawyer. Lesley had made some decisions and she would get things moving if she didn't hear from Dow by tomorrow. She wasn't going to put her life on hold any longer, hoping he'd come around. Suppose he didn't?

Thursday passed with no word and, on Friday, Lesley called Gael. She wanted to divide the rest of Gene's insurance money among the kids, she informed her, and she wanted to sell the house. The lawyer promised to start working on things the following Monday.

"I'll move in with Cass," she planned aloud, "if she will have me. Or I'll find myself an apartment in Queens where I'll be close enough to help Seth and Yoline with the baby sometimes. They can take whatever furniture they need to set up house, and I'll arrange to send Dow his piano. Generes will be happy to get her share of the sale; she can pay off her condo. If all goes well, I'll be out of here by Christmas."

She felt immensely relieved. Even if Cass didn't want her anymore, she was getting out of Westbury. Getting out of the past. She was more than a widow, more than a mother; she was a person. Dell was right, she thought. A person who needed her own life.

She picked up the phone again to invite Seth and Yoline to her own personal estate sale. Excitement revived within her.

41

Lesley called to make sure that Cass had, in fact, returned before she took the train into the City. She sounded warm and friendly and genuinely happy that Cass was back, but Cass would not let her own hopes soar. It could be that Lesley just wants to let you down gently, she cautioned herself.

She was not going to go gentle into that good night, however. She was absolutely not going to make it easy for Lesley. She would not coo sympathetically and say she understood that the kids must come first. And she was not going to wait any longer. Lesley had to decide tonight whether she stayed or left. She would not live suspended this way.

When the bell rang, Cass braced herself to be calm, cold, if absolutely necessary. But she could not prevent her cry of concern when Lesley walked through the apartment door. In four weeks, Lesley had lost all the weight they had joked about. And then some. For the first time she looked her age. Maybe even older.

"What's the matter?" Cass exclaimed, her resolutions summarily abandoned. "You've been sick!" she accused

Lesley shrugged. "No, I just haven't had much of an appetite lately." Her eyes roamed Cass's face and lingered on her lips, searching for the familiar gap. "I missed you, Cass," she said softly. "I feel like I haven't seen you in years."

"Yeah, I know what you mean," Cass admitted grudgingly.

She wanted to take Lesley's thin body into her arms and crush her, inhale her special smell, nuzzle the new hollows in her throat. But the fear of rejection held her back; she wasn't sure what footing their relationship was on now.

They stood a little awkwardly, just looking at each other.

"I'm sure you're hungry," Lesley said abruptly, hefting the bag she carried. "I know those airline meals are a joke." Provident as ever, she had brought dinner.

"I went first class, remember?" Cass reminded her.

Cass wasn't hungry; not for food, anyway. What she was hungry for was the way it used to be. The two of them here, around the table, talking inconsequentially as they ate. Comfortable in their routine. Confident that each was where she wanted to be. Happy that they were no more than yards away from the security and intimacy of their shared bed.

Lesley's appetite seemed to have suddenly returned, because she dug into the lasagna with relish and ate both heels of the garlic loaf. Rummaging around in the freezer, afterwards, she found a container of Ben and Jerry's ice cream. There wasn't much, and Cass, still amazed, declined.

Satisfied, Lesley sat listening quietly as Cass recounted her trip and relayed messages from the family. Then they went into the bedroom where Cass rummaged through her bags for various gifts the Shortmans had sent.

After she had examined and stacked her gifts, Lesley overturned Cass's suitcase and, like old times, began separating the clothes into neat piles. She held up a pair of jeans, frowning. "Clean or dirty?"

"It can take another wearing," Cass shrugged.

"I heard from Generes," Lesley slipped in casually.

"Really?" Cass tensed.

"Yes, she wrote to me."

"And?" Cass steeled herself.

"Well, she never mentioned you by name, but she alluded to our relationship as if it were in the past," Lesley admitted. "She said she hopes I meet 'someone nice.'"

Cass didn't flinch.

"She also said she was sorry at the way things turned out that night, and that she'd like us to forget it and start over."

That's pretty black of her," Cass said, regretting the sarcasm immediately as she heard Lesley sigh. "I'm sorry," she apologized. She held her breath. "And what did you say to her?"

Lesley paused. "I told her I'd already found someone nice, and I hoped she'd be as lucky some day."

Cass let her breath out slowly.

"I talked to Seth, too," Lesley continued. "I wanted to know why he was so calm, why he hadn't reacted like the others. He said that, at first, he thought I was seeing someone in the City ¾ a man, of course ¾ and you were simply covering for me. Which was fine by him, he said, because I seemed happy. He knew you were gay when he met you at Christmas, but he didn't know you were in love with me until after Generes disappeared with the car ..."

"What does that have to with it?" Cass broke in.

"Something about the way you looked at me and tried to keep things normal, he said. Anyway, the long and the short of it was that he said he loves me and he can understand why you would love me, too." She gave a lopsided smile. "Two out of three. Not bad."

She stuffed the dirty clothes in the hamper and came back to sit on the bed.

"Did Dell tell you we talked about me and you?"

"When?" Cass asked, bewildered. It was all too much. She was still trying to digest Seth's analysis and Generes's letter, for God's sake.

153

How did her sister-in-law become involved?

"The first time I called, your mother said you'd gone off with Luke, so I called there."

"Dell never told me you called. What'd she say?"

"We talked about my kids, first. Then about me and you ... things I already knew but needed to hear, I guess."

"I can't imagine Dell discussing me," Cass said in amazement. "I never met any woman who could mind her own business as well as Dell."

"Well, she obviously considers you her business," Lesley said dryly.

She shifted on the bed and impulsively grabbed Cass's arm. There was urgency in her voice. "Cass, I know you thought that things were over between us, and I'm sorry I went South on you. It's just that I was so concerned about what had happened with the kids. I was trying to look at things from their perspective, you know, especially Dow's. The fact that they had just lost their father. And, suddenly, it must seem like they're losing their mother, as well... .

"Death is fairly simple to understand, if not to accept. But this? Well, you have to admit: It's confusing. For God's sake, it's confusing for me ¾ and I've had time to think about it ¾ never mind them."

"What are you still confused about?" Cass inquired, eyes narrowed.

"Well, for one thing, I'm confused about whether I'm gay or not," Lesley burst out, throwing up her hands. "Don't take this the wrong way, Cass, but I really don't think that I am."

"I never thought you were," Cass stated.

"Which made me wonder if I may be bisexual," Lesley continued. "I don't even like that term, and I was never attracted to a woman before in my life! It's just so ... so *frustrating* being in the middle like this. People like to know what side of the fence you're on, and I *really* feel that I'm on the same old side ¾ except where you're concerned."

"But why do you feel you have to be on some 'side'?" Cass asked gently. "Why can't you just *be?* Don't you think I was confused by this, too? I'm gay. With a million other gay women to choose from, why did I have to fall in love with a straight woman and put myself through this? Why? I don't understand it, but I've come to accept it. I love *you*, Lesley. I don't love straight women. Just you."

"You know," Lesley said thoughtfully, "I never looked at it like that before. I really never did. And you're right. Why me? You could've been with someone who had no kids, no complications. But you know what, Cass? I'm glad it *is* me and I'm glad it's you, too."

She smiled. "Remember what you said to me on your birthday, Cass, that day in Mystic?"

"Of course, I remember."

"You still feel that way?"

"A lot of things have changed, pet, but not that," Cass asserted. "I still feel the same way about you."

"I hoped you would, because I'd like to start wearing the ring you gave me."

She splayed her fingers, and Cass noticed for the first time that her fingers were bare. "I put away my wedding ring, and I gave Seth the others. Yoline never got an engagement ring, and I thought she'd like a diamond; she deserves it. Seth said he'll keep the anniversary band and see how things go." She smiled. "I think things'll go."

"I think so, too. They seem to be good for each other."

Like we are, Lesley thought.

Maybe there's no word for what I am, but I know the word for what we feel. It's called love. As long as we're human, there are always possibilities.

42

The leaves were barely turning, but there was definitely a chill to the September day. They let themselves in and the door squeaked a bit. It had been weeks since Lesley was last here.

The movers had already taken most of the downstairs furniture, and the rooms had that funny, hollow quality. Cass thought it was a riot and deliberately raised her voice just so she could hear her echo.

The kitchen, however, was intact. They were going to pack the major pieces for storage until they were ready to ship their things to Antigua. They would take the smaller items to Cass's apartment. Correction: their apartment.

They were also here for closure. Lesley had decided it was necessary that Cass spend a night with her ¾with her¾ in this house before it was sold. She had to correct the outsider status that Cass associated with the place. And Cass, though hesitant, understood it was important that they lay this ghost to rest together.

Lesley kept the conversation centered on them, refusing to visit the incident of two months ago. They talked of how cramped they were going to be when they got all of her clothes and books to the City, and they discussed the possibility of moving to a larger place, perhaps in Astoria or Park Slope.

"I tell you: I'd rather be cramped in a studio with you than be alone in a mansion," Cass declared. "I'm not letting you out of my sight again."

"Don't worry, I've burned my bridges now," Lesley answered. "You won't be able to get rid of me."

By the time they were done, they were exhausted and dirty, and Cass suggested they get some Chinese takeout. But Lesley insisted on doing things right, and they drove to the store to get supper and breakfast fixings.

In short order, they whipped up a meal of chicken stir fry with noodles. Then while Cass showered, Lesley took a bottle of wine from the liquor cabinet and stuck it in the freezer, annoyed at herself for not chilling it sooner. She made up for it by rummaging around in the sideboard (Seth had no room for it), where she found a pair of candles. Why not go all the way? She went outside where hydrangea bushes hugged the sun porch and cut a couple of the purple-blue heads. They were a bit dry, but they'd do.

"Now, we're in business," she said to herself, surveying the little table with satisfaction.

The evening had all the makings of a date, and since they had no further to go than upstairs, they finished the bottle of wine. With a couple of ice cubes, it tasted really fine. When Cass proposed they dance, it seemed perfectly reasonable, and bringing the kitchen radio into the empty living room, they swayed to the music of an oldies station, softly singing the lyrics of their youth into each other's ears.

Later they undressed for bed, Cass with a little trepidation, Lesley with equanimity. The picture of Gene had been taken down and stored with Lesley's special things in the basement of her parents' house.

Naked and warm from the wine, they were content to nestle in the darkness. We're home, Lesley thought, as she drifted off. Wherever we're together, we're at home. She smiled into the brown space between her lover's shoulders.

Cass, too, was smiling. Tomorrow she would finally see the sun color her woman's body in the morning's new light.

******

That Nina, Cass thought, mmm-hmm! Throwing the magazine aside, she joined Lesley in song:

... To the top, right-hand corner of the ceiling in my room,
Where we'll stay, until the sun shines another day
To swing on clotheslines ...
May I be always
In the morning of my liiiife.

"Pity you got rid of the piano," Cass chuckled, as the song ended. "I think we've got quite an act here."

"A little practice and we'll take it on the road," Lesley retorted.

They could've lain there all day, but they had to get back to the City to prepare for work next morning. Reluctantly, they got up, gathered their things and loaded the car.

This was goodbye, Lesley knew, even though she would return to the house until it was sold. Suddenly, she was overwhelmed by sadness. She had spent most of her married life here and had raised her children in this house. From a cheap foreclosure, they had turned it into a real home. From this front door, she had stepped out to attend Generes's tennis matches, Dow's recitals, Seth's races. And Gene's funeral. All her adult memories, good and bad, were concentrated in this house.

Now they were all gone: Gene, Generes, Dow and Seth. Dow was twice gone, she sighed, from this house and from her life. His absence still hurt, an ongoing pain that was dulled but not eliminated. But this part of her life was written. It was time for her to go, too.

Fiddling with the keys, she cast a last, watery glance over the front of the house. She heard the phone ring faintly. Rolling her eyes at Cass, she began to unlock the door.

"Bet you by the time I get there it stops," she said. She really felt like letting it ring, but the thought occurred to her that it very well could be Dow. Sudden haste made thumbs of her fingers, and Cass took the keys from her and opened the door. She had not missed Lesley's tears.

The phone still pealed as Lesley ran through to the kitchen, and she fumbled the receiver in the gathering darkness.

"Hello?" she said cautiously, a question in her voice.

"Mom!" It was Seth, and her heart settled in guilty disappointment.

"Hi, hon. You just caught me."

"Good thing!" he exclaimed. "Good thing, Grandma!"

Grandma? Did he say Grandma?

"Cass," she screamed, in excitement.

Fear hobbling her legs, Cass struggled to move indoors, to make her way to the kitchen where she could make out Lesley jumping up and down.

"What?" she gasped.

"The baby! The baby's here."

Lesley shouted back into the phone. "What is it? A boy? A boy! Yes, yes," she turned, nodding, to relay the news to Cass. "About 30 minutes ago. Eight pounds, two; twenty-one inches. Oooh, that's a big one!" she babbled happily.

"How's Yoline?" Cass whispered, prompting her.

"How's Yoline?" Lesley asked Seth.

"Fine," she reported back. "Tired. In recovery. She was in labor since this morning, but she wasn't certain, because the baby's due date isn't for a couple weeks." Then to Seth: "Can we come? We're on our way back to the City, anyway. OK. OK. We'll drive fast and make it before visiting hours are over. Great! Congratulations, hon! Oh, wait! What's his name? Good, good. OK. See you soon.

"His name is Nigel Eugene Gorton, in memory of his grandfathers," Lesley announced proudly.

"That's a good name. Strong. Manly. Like his dad," Cass declared. She took Lesley gently by the chin. "Let me be the first to kiss the world's sexiest grandmother," she said, kissing her lips.

Linking hands, they left the house again. This time, they did not look back. Driving into the sun, their minds were on the future. And, yes, it was full of possibilities.

THE END